HUMAN INTERACTIONS

(Can We Improve Them?)

Theoretical and Practical Challenges
for this Newly-born
Century/Millennium

Walter F.R. Ribeiro

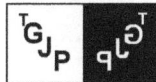

A Gestalt Journal Press Publication

Gestalt Therapy on the World Wide Web

The Gestalt Therapy Page is the Internet's oldest and most comprehensive web resource for information, resources, and publications relating to the theory and practice of Gestalt therapy.

Visitors can subscribe to News and Notes, a free email calendar of conferences, training programs, and other events of interest to the worldwide Gestalt therapy community.

The Gestalt Therapy Page includes an on-line store that offers the most comprehensive collection of books and recordings available – many available nowhere else!

Visit today: www.gestalt.org

The Gestalt Journal Press was founded in 1975 and is currently the leading publisher and distributor of books, journals, and educational recordings relating to the theory and practice of Gestalt therapy. Our list of titles includes new editions of all the classic works by Frederick Perls, Laura Perls, Paul Goodman, Ralph Hefferline, and Jan Christiaan Smuts. Our catalog also includes a wide variety of books by contemporary theoreticians and clinicians including Richard Hycner, Lynne Jacobs, Violet Oaklander, Peter Phillipson, Erving & Miriam Polster, Edward W. L. Smith, and Gary Yontef.

In 1976, we began publication of The Gestalt Journal (now the International Gestalt Journal), the first professional periodical devoted exclusively to the theory and practice of Gestalt therapy.

Our collection of video and audio recordings features the works of Frederick (Fritz) and Laura Perls, Violet Oaklander, Erving & Miriam Polster, Janie Rhyne, and James Simkin.

The Gestalt Journal Press, in conjunction with the University of California, Santa Barbara, maintains the world's largest archive of Gestalt therapy related materials including original manuscripts and correspondence, published and unpublished, by Gestalt therapy pioneers Frederick & Laura Perls and Paul Goodman. The archives also include more than six thousand hours of audio and video recordings of presentations, panels and interviews dating to early 1961.

Translated by Fernando Rosa Ribeiro
And Priscila Maria Magaldi-Netto (the appendices)

TO ALL OF US:

DOMINATORS/DOMINATED

OPPRESSORS/OPPRESSED

VICTIMS/VICTIMIZERS (TORTURERS)

THE VIOLENT /THE FRIGHTENED(SCARED)

(Specially to Elayne, Helena Raíra, Luiz Fernando and Marina) that, in different degrees, have dreamed of a world where interactions will be more loving and humane.

My warmest acknowledgments to my masters/friends:

Gary Yontef

and

Michael Vincent Miller

PRECONCEPTIONS — ALWAYS IN THE PLURAL —

WERE HISTORICALLY CREATED,

BUT ARE NONETHELESS ROOTED IN ALL OF US,

INDIVIDUALLY.

THERE IS NO EASY WAY OUT HERE.

Fernando Rosa Ribeiro
Anthropologist

TABLE OF CONTENTS

Being-in-Relation: Putting the Interactional or Pheno-menological Therapies Into Context
The Quality of Our Interactionships and Their Consequences
How Our Being Had To Adjust, Organize And Develop Himself In Order To Survive In Generally Very Adverse Contexts
Sense and Importance of the Concept of Resistance
Healing: What is That?
The Non-Paradoxical Theory of Change
A Critique of the Instruments (Processes) Centered on "Doing"
What Should Be Done?
Cognition and Existence Are One and the Same Thing. So, to Transmit it Has it's Own Way.

PREFACE

Walter Ribiero is on fire. His writing lives and breathes his fierce commitment to the free development of one's being, and a fierce resistance to conformity and submission. He should know about such things, having grown up and lived through the times of corrupt authoritarian, dictatorial rule in Brazil. He has lived to see the transition to a more democratic state, with the personal and political liberations that democratic processes foster. However, it is a condition new enough that it is not taken for granted.

Many of us for whom English is a first language have grown complacent. With generations of relative democracy and relative economic security under our belts, we lose sight of the fragility of subjectivity. Ribiero knows first-hand how repressive political and social structures impinge on the free-play of our awareness, impinge on the expansion of our experiential world.

Is it any wonder that the founders of Gestalt therapy were cultural and political outsiders? They too knew first-hand the intimate interplay between personal and political freedoms, and they decried the subtle and gross repressive forces that continually threaten free thought, even in democracies. Ribiero lives in a new democracy, in a state in which free thought is a hard-won gain. Most native English speakers live in long-established democracies, but we are in a time where once again there are subtle and gross pressures for conformity of thought, speech and action at every level of government and society.

Ribiero's experience with authoritarian rule, with its pressures to conform and submit, have fueled his passion for reminding us of the existential thrust of our theory. The existential thrust is the guardian of our individuality and of our freely flowing process of awareness.

In our post-Cartesian, contextualist age, the question of individuality is often confused with individualism. Ribiero is no champion of the very Western notion of individualism. He does champion individual conscience and the courage to be aware and think freely. But he shows very clearly, in his orientation and in his clinical examples, that our familial, social and political contexts are crucial factors that limit or enhance such capacities. What he underscores is the necessity to rise to the challenge of keeping our free awareness alive. We must see ourselves as part of the society that can enhance or inhibit our psychological freedoms, and in so doing we are no longer mere victims of the society "out there," but co-participants in keeping freedom alive for all of us.

Ribiero tells you — in a charmingly disarming manner that characterizes many passages in this book — that he is truly a child of Brazil: a man of poor country origins.

> "I am a caipira or country bumpkin from
> the interior of São Paulo State, and,

therefore, a Jeca or hillbilly, as one of our writers, Antônio Callado, put it. I mention it just as a reminder that it is not with impunity that we are born in a given place and at a point in time. That is, our personal history, the history of our ancestors the point in time in which we live, speak of us. They talk of what we know, of our idiosyncrasy, of the prejudices we have that always influence us in one way or another. In the same way, history is the deciding factor in order to understand society and its problems.

Besides my *Jeca*-style, I think it is important to mention that the fact that I am Brazilian makes me less rational than, for instance, a Frenchman, and less pragmatic than, for instance, an American."

Thus his story begins. The reader is immediately taken into a world that lives and breathes, and draws no sharp boundaries between the personal, the political and the social realms. And much credit is due the translators, who have managed to translate the lyric poeticism of Ribiero's style.

What Ribiero does not tell you is that he is now highly educated, philosophically astute, highly esteemed, and considered by many to be the "father" of Gestalt therapy and theory in Brazil. He has certainly nurtured the Brazilian Gestalt therapy "baby" from its earliest days onward with care, with dedication, with education and training, with exhortation and argument, and finally, with the shining quality of his presence. Brazil now has a thriving Gestalt community, richly diverse in thought and practice, alive with the squabbles and rivalries and loves of an extended family, one that owes a debt to this man and his writings. These inspiring writings are finally making their way to the English-speaking Gestalt world in the September of his life.

— Lynne Jacobs, Ph.D.
Los Angeles, 2005

INTRODUCTION

I am a caipira or country bumpkin from the interior of São Paulo State, and, therefore, a Jeca or hillbilly, as one of our writers, Antônio Callado, put it. I mention it just as a reminder that it is not with impunity that we are born in a given place and at a point in time. That is, our personal history, the history of our ancestors the point in time in which we live, speak of us. They talk of what we know, of our idiosyncrasy, of the prejudices we have that always influence us in one way or another. In the same way, history is the deciding factor in order to understand society and its problems.

Besides my *Jeca*-style, I think it is important to mention that the fact that I am Brazilian makes me less rational than, for instance, a Frenchman, and less pragmatic than, for instance, an American.

That is a valuable advantage in order to understand approaches that also stress the right hemisphere, as ours do. As for the remainder of my prejudices, they are, unsurprisingly, not very far from the classic prejudices inflicted on the citizens of other parts of this world of ours. A world that is increasingly homogenized, conflict-ridden and full of ready-made truths.

Besides those mentioned above, I have been heavily influenced by my first educator, my unhappy mother (how original of me). She was a woman who was as intelligent

---

1

as she was full of sorrow and resentment because she did not belong any more to the decadent landed elite of her time. She directed her resentment particularly at men, and especially at her father. He would have squandered the family heirloom. But she also directed it at my father, who was neither brilliant nor had the drive to give back to her the station that was hers "by right and birth."

Thus, since the first moment I got the message that I should be different. I should be the "savior" of all oppressed womankind, and not only of her or my sister. That, obviously, would leave a mark not only on my view of the world but also on my encounters/misencounters with women. Any first-year student of psychology is able to guess as much.

Of course, being a trained savior was also responsible for my choosing my profession.

From this background, wandering through philosophy and psychology, I have always preferred the more holistic (interactionist) views as regards defining the human being and dealing with him. For instance, in 1963, I was asked to write a paper where I would define man on the basis of a given bibliography. This last was made up of psychoanalytic, behaviorist and Gestalt psychology's perspectives. My paper visibly veered to the last of the three. Since then, I have gone further in that direction.

This stance, in one way or another, brings into proximity some approaches that come under different names. All of them however conceive the human being on the basis of the same ontology, showing us, in this way, the essence and intention of their basic assumptions. I believe that many of the differences shown by those approaches are marginal.

I am aware today of the great debt we all owe to:

Phenomenology as developed by the later Husserl and Merleau-Ponty. It is the indispensable philosophical basis to all those revolutionary forms of conceiving and dealing with the human being;

The recent Biology of Cognition initiated by Humberto Maturana Romencin and Francisco José Varela;

The decisive stance against the "OR"s and in favor of the "AND"s. This has helped Gestalt therapy's process of acceptance (healing). Its brilliant etiology of neurosis and insights on human functioning were mainly put forward in the main work of Perls et al. (1994);

The poignant denunciation of the violence with which society (through its authoritarian representatives: parents, teachers, doctors, psychotherapists, etc) has deformed us so as to impose its norms on us, mainly through Alice Miller's work (1997, 1993 and 1984a);

Carl Rogers and his great contribution through his person-centered approach. Foremost are his concepts of "unconditional, positive consideration for the person" and his related concept of "freedom to learn." This last was also developed by A S. Neil and his outstanding educational experiment (Summerhill). The experiment is now, decades later, under the responsibility of his daughter in England;

The liberating pedagogical philosophy of Paulo Freire;

The latest experiments on motivation that have led Deci (1996) to ascertain differences in performance results when there is *control* and *coercion* and when there is *"support for autonomy;"*

The sensibility of artists, writers, playwrights, filmmakers and, above all, of poets such as, for instance, Fernando Pessoa.

I have mentioned those whom I remember most strongly and to whom I am grateful. I am aware of the extent to which they have opened my eyes and of how much they have influenced me in my adoption and development of my stance. I apologize for omitting the names of the many other people to whom I surely owe a lot because of their influence in more than thirty years of search. However, among these I cannot fail to mention:

Introduction

Thérèse A. Tellegen: in the beginning of 1972, she was fresh from London, where she had taken part in two demonstration workshops. She set up, with Thereza (Tessy) Hantzschel, Jean Clark Juliano, myself and one or two other people, a Gestalt therapy study group. From then on, a few Gestalt therapists and, importantly, the approach's basic book, that by Perls et al. (1995), have given me invaluable support, elucidation and lots of headaches. Headaches that now I am sharing with you (sorry . . .).

If we agree with the contents and the essence of the radical ideas, experiments and proposals of those thinkers that have been influencing consistently, the modern history of thinking about the human being and especially education and psychotherapy, we should then ask: how is it possible that — and why — such basic ideas about the human being's nature, his conditions and possibilities of cognition and interactions "still wander down the back roads of contemporary psychology and psychotherapy?" (In the words of Michael Vincent Miller on Gestalt therapy, in his new introduction to Perls et al., 1994: viii).

In their Introduction in Perls et al. (1994) the authors had already written:

"Indispensable — both for the writing and the thorough understanding of this book — is an attitude which as a theory actually permeates the contents and method of the

book. Thus the reader is apparently confronted with an impossible task: to understand the book, he must have the 'Gestaltist' mentality, and to acquire it he must understand the Book."

Husserl, himself, had stated: "the phenomenon only can be accessed through the phenomenological method," (Of course, the Perls et al. statement, though true, is the result of the authors' grandiosity when they ascribe to themselves only a "mentality" that they learned from their teachers, who would surely have preferred to call it phenomenological).

This is a crucial statement. It is good for all the approaches that we call interactional. However, it stands in the way of our haste, our need to solve "problems" quickly, and so it has been passed over by almost all of us. This is so because it deeply affects our grandiosity when it suggests, so emphatically, a general characterological difficulty to enter in contact with and genuinely understand new and revolutionary proposals, particularly when these conflict so much with our old beliefs and prejudices.

The statement inconveniently points to a great conflict between our deep-rooted older beliefs, our most performing classic prejudices about what is the human being, and the proposal, the revolutionary reading of what is the human being that is being put forward.

What we have in all known so-called civilized societies is a very ancient conception, which is the result of **authori-**

tarian thinking. According to it, the human being is in the wrong already at birth. He is the bearer of the original sin and full of instincts and impulses that are not reliable and that need to be controlled and/or corrected by "educators" from the society to which he belongs. History however tells us that there have always come up people who have put in check those old beliefs. It also tells us that such challenges — in one way or another — have been passed over and their authors have also been, in one way or another, ignored and/or persecuted.

Considering this deep-rooted and endemic belief (disbelief), nothing is more natural than the development and idolizing of the cane and "dark pedagogy" (Alice Miller, 1984a), as the universal, absolute and vital instruments of "education." and child upbringing. We should identify the cane with education's thousand faces, colors and tints. **The conflict of beliefs at work here is clear.** If we believe in the need to use the cane (punishment/reinforcement, support/frustration, chastisement/incentive, competition, just to mention the most frequent forms it takes), it is clear and obvious that we do not believe in the potentialities of the human being when this last is free, accepted and confirmed. If, on the other hand, we believe that he in fact only moves on the basis of intrinsic motivation, and that this last only comes up in freedom and acceptance, we cannot believe in any of the changed faces of authoritarianism and its canes.

Because we are social beings, there is a first great paradox we have to deal with (as emphasized by Perls et al.,

1994, especially Chapter VI). This is the existing conflict between the society that we need to create in order to be confirmed in it, in order to develop our potentialities and live out our essentiality as independent and auto-creating beings (besides phenomenological ontology, see Maturana e Varela, 1987/1995), and the disconfirming society, authoritarian, un-nurturing, and with scant love and acceptance. This society is already there, created by others, the product of a long history of wars, conflicts and struggle for power (no matter how insignificant this last might be). This society is imposed on us "ready and made;" therefore, it is not willing to reexamine itself, nor doubt its confusing and often-outdated values.

I will try to reflect throughout this short book on the roots of this alienating dichotomization and the resulting conflicts. These have put out roots and developed inside our history and inside us much earlier than I had thought at first.

Those conflicts have generated so much difficulty in understanding that I wonder (suspect) whether this view, so radically democratic, of the interactions, formation and development of the human being, would not yet be too new for the autocracy that stills governs and influences us.

However, this bitterly realistic picture cannot be discarded unless we keep wearing our visors. We hope that the many lights — brought particularly in the last century by psychologists, physicists, biologists and thinkers as the ones mentioned above — will illuminate a little more people in the future. We also hope that they will give them the courage needed to look inside and outside of them. This in order to identify the prepotency around us. The prepotency that erodes and corrupts our relationships, makes difficult and even destroys our ability to notice and accept the new, the different, in spite of the clearness with which they generally present themselves to us.

Would an approach that really takes the side of the humane and not of the historically pre-established norms, therefore, be an approach only possible in a radical way at the end of this new century? We fear so, considering the great obstacles, resistance and "misunderstandings" that these proposals have encountered in their — not only rational — understanding, and in their large scale practice. **In fact, those proposals pull the rug from under our feet, the ground of the old authoritarian myths, of the pseudo-certainties and illusory security**. Therefore, they are very threatening to our precarious and paralyzing adjustments.

Do we really need so much pessimism in order to wake us up? Does the "noise" from those ideas still irritate us like an alarm clock early in the morning? Perls repeated endlessly that you do not grow without suffering. Bornheim (1973) tells us that it is negative experience that allows us to free ourselves from dogmas; and Alice Miller (1997, chapter II) tells us that the grandiose is stuck to his grandiosity and can only free himself if depression gets him. Here seem to be some of the more serious reasons for our avoidance, the gaps mentioned by Perls and the constant denials mentioned so often by Alice Miller. Will this be the great challenge of this century? Does "The Liberating Experience of Facing the Painful Truth" (A. Miller, 1993, subtitle) still frighten us so much? My rage at coming in touch with some of those ideas strongly suggests so, even though that is the same rage of some of the people with whom I share those ideas.

Anyway, such a picture of utter stubbornness and/or resistance in the face of such obvious and clear statements is intriguing. It incites us to look for more serious motives than mere difficulty in intellectual understanding to absorb them.

As from 1980 I have had resource to Maurice Merleau Ponty and the phenomenological method in order to rethink those approaches. And, obviously, also in order to review and rethink the book that at first stimulated me the most: *Gestalt Therapy*, by Perls et al., 1951/1994. This is a book that has been as often quoted by Gestalt practitioners as it has been little read and even less understood by us.

I began to give lectures about my first findings and particularly about my doubts. Those lectures made many in the therapeutic community uncomfortable; especially because I put forward many issues, many doubts and no answers.

Of course, those uncertainties, those doubts generate insecurity that, in turn, calls up defensiveness and resistance. They rigidify character and therefore make comprehension of theory even more difficult: "fundamental theoretical errors are invariably characterological, the result of a neurotic failure of perception, feeling or action," wrote Perls et al., 1994, chapter II, 6. Those are mistakes that, for these reasons, besides being cruel, it is also useless to try to confront.

However, as I was scared by that lack of fit between theory and our practice, I delved into the matter, even though somewhat awkwardly. I believe that awkwardness caused those with whom I shared my doubts to receive the news too suddenly. Apparently, in this way they lost the ground under their feet and became even more scared than I. Worse, some began to become really defensive. The matter is irksome, and my discourse was very harsh (how could it not be?), unintentionally or not. Of course, my scant attention to the delicacy with which we should treat the matter (mainly due to my own insufficient absorption of theory) made matters worse.

I cannot insist too much that the work of those I mentioned above, that are my main masters, has always been the vital support on this shifting ground, besides, naturally, the work of the many others that have dealt with the problem and rethought it.

I believe that the findings of those pioneers have generated — besides unrestricted enthusiasm — extremely strong resistance/denials, particularly unconscious ones. This belief of mine has been largely confirmed. On the other hand, the spectacular sale figures for their books brighten us up because it seems a sign that a growing number of people is beginning to develop the existential support that is needed to do away with their visors.

In what concerns practice, a workshop in which I took part in the States had a precious finding in store for me: the style, the therapeutic attitude on live that I experienced in my encounter with Irma Shepherd. Her stance when faced with the trainees and/or clients or any other person was for me an example of non-defensive interactions, of utter, naked acceptance. One talks a lot about those relations and recommends them, but they are seldom seen.

This and other examples of therapeutic work are of the highest level of clinical sophistication. They have obtained fully satisfactory results that are easily empirically corroborated. They stimulate us and are in sharp contrast with the overwhelming majority of examples of work that seem to me to be either merely cathartic or problem-centered and, therefore, only role-producing. The person is relieved, develops a few abilities and, feeling obviously a little better, goes on being basically the same, taking advantage of every opportunity towards self-conquest and to get away from himself more and more. **That is, he develops the abilities and the readiness to eliminate conflict through self-alienation,** through an attempt at self-repression or even suppression of part of himself. The growing alienation is effective because it is also elaborated by constant experiences often put forward as "therapeutic."

Introduction

Repeated, constant and careful reading, mainly of the works quoted, corroborates and gives support to more permissive and accepting attitudes. Relying on those readings and examples, we have been developing a way of evaluating the types of related attitudes witnessed in psychotherapeutic situations or other interactions. We have also been intensifying the search for possible basic beliefs that could provide them with support and meaning. Fortunately, another science, the Biology of Cognition, has reached the same beliefs.

Bearing that in mind, we have sought to reach the intentional core of those approaches and the essence of their beliefs and basic propositions. And, on that foundation, we have sought to get to the intention that guides or should guide the way of being and, therefore, the attitudes and work of their followers.

Since then our work has been to mark out with growing accuracy which kinds of attitude in interactions lead one way (the confirming, the "therapeutic") and which lead the other way (for instance, the disconfirming, the role-producer). This arduous but gratifying work is intended as a contribution to emphasizing and, up to a certain point, clarifying this crucial problem for the practice of our profession, especially for those who have adopted our approaches.

In the beginning of the book, the emphasis is laid on the attempt to understand and explain what is the human being for those who see him as we do. When we begin to understand that, we seek to understand how he reacts to stimuli around him: how he moulds himself in his interactions and, with that organization in place, how he perceives and "responds" to the world and others. That is, we try to understand the roots of our existential stance and what has led us to it; what we are in terms of the existential struggles we have had to face in order to survive in the best possible way in those contexts that are almost always adverse.

The emphasis on the inevitability of our development being the result of that constant struggle for the "best" way to survive has grown with the book. Noticing that has compelled us to face in a completely new way the instances of "resistance," "defenses," "neuroses," or any other kind of "deviation" or blockage. We have always tried to take the radicalness of the proposals of our teachers as far as our limitations will allow.

From Chapter V to Chapter VII, I try to draw on what is obvious about healing and treatment from the perspective of trust in the abilities/potentialities of the human being. Further, I call attention to the fact that the other side, the side of molding (whatever strategies may have been used) is the result of authoritarian thinking and the lack of belief in the potentialities of the human being. That inevitably has led us to get further away from ourselves, our longings and emotions, separating us from our volition and our will.

In Annex I put forward the obvious notion that we can only transmit those ideas if we behave, during the process of teaching, in a way that is as close as is possible for us to the precepts that we preach.

References:

Bornheim, Gerd — Introduction to Philosophize (The Philosophical Thinking on Existential Basis) — Ed. Globo, Porto Alegre, RS, Brazil

Deci, Edward L. 1996. *Why We Do What We Do — Understanding Self-Motivation.* Penguin: NY.

Miller, A. 1994. *The Drama of the Gifted Child.* Basic Books: NY.

Miller, A. 1994. *The Search for the True Self.* Basic Books: NY.

Miller, A. 1983. *For Your Own Good* (Hidden cruelty in child-rearing and the roots of violence), Farrar-Strauss-Giroux: NY.

Miller, A. 1993. *Breaking Down the Wall of Silence* (The Liberating Experience of Facing Painful Truth. A Meridien Book, Penguin Press: NY.

Perls, F.S.; Hefferline, R.; Goodman, P. 1994. *Gestalt Therapy: Excitement and Growth in the Human Personality.* The Gestalt Journal Press: Gouldsboro,: ME.

Merleau-Ponty, Maurice — "Les Cours de Sorbonne, Les Sciences de L'homme et la Phénoménologie" — Centre de Documentation Universitaire — 5, Place de La Sorbone, Paris V.

Maturana R., Humberto and Varela, Francisco. 1995. "The Tree of Knowledge" First edition Scherz Verlag, Berna, Munique and Viena (1987). Brazilian edition, *Editorial Psy.*

See bibliography for others' works of Biology of Cognition. This last, I think, solidifies and enrich the phenomenological ontology and method of the later Husserl (developed by Merleau-Ponty) that are our main philosophical source.

Any theoretical point of view or practice deriving from it, in order to be understood, must be seen under the light of its context and harmonized with it.

CHAPTER I

Being-in-Relation: Putting the Interactional or Phenomenologically-Inspired Therapies Into Context

In order to understand better what is happening with the evolution of psychotherapy today, it is essential that we study the evolution of paradigms used to understand the human being and, as a consequence, the possibilities, difficulties and limitations imposed by working with them.

This is perhaps a greater problem in the approaches that are by vocation and essence unfinished, such as the one we embrace and defend. Furthermore, their scientific/philosophical paradigm still fight against scientist or essentialist paradigms, in spite of the fact that the model of those "scientists" has been overcome on almost all scientific fronts, first of all in physics and nowadays also in neurobiology.

We are part of the great artistic/scientific/philosophical movement that became stronger in the turn of the twentieth century. It aimed (and stills aims) at overcoming the mechanist thought of the nineteenth century. It is a movement of thinking that happened notably in Continental Europe.

This movement came up and was deeply rooted there. It has spread and developed all over the world. Because of that it has had to face many shocks with different cultures and kinds of thinking that have been often radically opposed to it. This difficulty seems to have gone unnoticed or has been avoided by all the theoreticians that have thought up new forms of psychotherapy.

In psychology, Carl Rogers has been the great exception. His training in American logical positivism could not prevent (as it does in the case of the majority of other psychologists) that his exceptional sensibility perceived the human being in a direct way (and therefore without the mediation of previous pre-conceptions) throughout his extensive and intensive contact with people. This stance and that kind of contact made it possible for him to perceive which kind of relation make people shrink, disguise or defend themselves, thereby keeping and/or intensifying the neuroses, and which kind of relation leads them the other way, the way of cure.

With that unusual ability, and based on empirical data, he came close to the essence of human behavior. Not by chance or coincidence, that is the same essence to which came great European theoreticians through theoretical paths.

In this way, with set foundations for his theory and practice, Rogers said, when he came into contact with Existential Phenomenology:

I was surprised to find, around 1951, that the direction of my thought and the central aspects of my therapeutic work could rightly be classified as existential and pheno-menological. It seems strange that an American psychologist could find himself in such company.(Amatuzzi, 1989, p. 91)

This happy encounter between a confirmed practice with theory gives us solace and encourages us. Of course, it also worries us as we see thousands of people imitating Rogers without his sensibility or genius, on the one hand, and, on the other hand, without any theory that gives support to their practice. The disaster has been inevitable because, after all, the Rogers are extremely rare in this world. Even though we cannot forget that Rogers' "person-centered" concept *"prevents him from reaching a phenomenological type of therapy, a tendency that we see in the evolution of his work"* (Moreira, 1993).

Gestalt therapy, as we know, came directly out of the German theoretical point of view. That is why Laura Perls, for instance, would call the two Pauls (Goodman and Weiz) Europeans or Renaissance men. They were both very rare in America, according to her (Rosenblatt 1991).

We know that those geniuses faced (and still face) strong opposition. That opposition is based on values and beliefs that are profoundly ingrained in all of us. That makes each one of us into oppositionists that are more or less unaware of those ideas. [Whenever we have some

---

idea of that resistance (as when we begin to become aware, as Gestalt therapists say) and, overcoming denial, accept the existence of the defensiveness of that inner oppositionist, we take away some of his power].

Another aggravating factor: we psychologists, due to the exclusive emphasis for so many years on the **intra** aspect, are still in general neglectful or little competent to consider the power of cultural and environmental differences and prejudices. This in spite of all that has been done in the past few years in several sciences and psychological approaches to counterbalance that earlier exaggerated emphasis.

With the aim of only sketching the problem, let us go back to the last years of the nineteenth century and the first years of this one. That was when the systematization of the fight between different opinions intensified. Those opinions were divided (as they still are unbelievably to this day) between two equally essentializing positions. We can call them, for simplicity's sake, the **subjectivist** and **objectivist** positions. It was an old war that would become stronger at that time.

The main novelty then was the systematization of the view that later Maslow would call the Third Force, notably as carried out chiefly by the mathematician and philosopher Edmond Husserl, the "founder of Phenomenology in the modern sense" (M. Merleau-Ponti, 1973:19). That movement would influence all branches of European culture and, of course, psychology, psychiatry and neurology. Next, it would spread all over the world.

That influence reached, for instance, the first creators of Gestalt therapy that got their training (formation) in that period and in that atmosphere. It exerted itself directly through the Gestalt psychologists and perhaps even more through Kurt Goldstein, and indirectly through all continental European culture of the time.

Concerning this atmosphere of cultural ebullience, Maurice Merleau-Ponty would say later (1973:20): "We can say that all that was done in Germany from 1915/1920 was directly or indirectly under the influence of phenomenology and courses given by Husserl were enough to explain it." Moreover, Heidbreder (1964:487) says: "The understanding of the most important contemporary psychological currents and ultimately all attempts to place the psychic issue within clear and ordered perspectives will not be achieved without the knowledge of phenomenology as elaborated by Husserl."

Therefore, not taking seriously the obviousness of that influence and of that affiliation is to behave dangerously like an ostrich.

One of the forms of denial, maybe the most dangerous, is speedy and superficial acceptance only on the level of rational opinion. For instance, it is stressed again and again that we are phenomenological/existential. However, the vast majority of the authors of that statement have a very superficial notion — if they have one at all —

of what is this way of thinking and conceiving the human being. They do not go back to the origins to really learn what they are actually talking about or, if they do, they do so only with their rational thinking. This last is not enough to understand our approaches (Phenomenology is only accessible through the phenomenological method).

In the last decades, our notion about the human being's nature, functioning and development received a powerful ally in Biology of Cognition that reaches at an almost equal Ontology, for instance, Merleau-Ponty's Ontology in "Visible and Invisible."

An integral part of this movement, and maybe the greatest merit, for instance, of Gestalt therapy, is the stance of denouncement and fight against conflicting dualities; its firm positioning against the OR's and decisive adherence to the AND's. We are this AND that, conscience AND body, reason AND emotion, and so forth. In that way, it touches in a practical manner the crucial issue of our devising of our concept of normalcy. At the same time, it touches on how the process of deviation and/or interruption works in normal growth; how, furthermore, it makes possible the creation of powerful clinical tools like the attitude of clear and confirming comprehension that makes possible the personal work of creative integration of conflicting polarities.

Fortunately for us, we do not need to become philosophers, physicists or biologists in order to have what we need to develop a phenomenological view of the Human

Being in Relation

Being and the World. In the beginning, it is enough that we do not forget that we are not the issue of spontaneous birth and that nobody has genial insights based on nothing.

That does not exist. Nobody takes something out of nothing. Every cultural movement of any kind only develops from a certain previous maturing. It needs ground and a certain state of readiness provided by its historical moment or the historical moment of the evolution of culture in order that it can be felt and thought up, in order that it can be brought to light. Needless to say, those movements bring up a great deal of defensiveness.

In that way thinkers are those who catch the fundamental issues of their historical moment and reflect on them. They suggest some times a few solutions that at the moment of their presentation are hardly understood, let alone accepted. That is because they often conflict with the conservative pre-conceptions of the time.

The artist, usually through his intuition, seems to catch that atmosphere of readiness even before scientists and philosophers. The best example I can find of a view of the human being and the world such as ours is in some way prior to the elaboration and systematization carried out by the great thinkers, is the work of the Portuguese poet, Fernando Pessoa. In his work, it is striking the difference between the worlds in which each one lives in function of different perspectives and the resulting emotions that arise in each of them at each moment and vice versa, in a process of constant feedback. The poet divided himself into four characters in order to sign his work. We like to say that the poems signed by him when he felt he was Alberto Caieiro were written when his view and feelings about the I, the Other and the world were very close to ours.

Of course, he also did not get that out of anything. Besides his unique poetic vocation, he was tuned to the problems and attempts at solution suggested in his time. He was tuned to the readiness of his historical moment and, in order to be up to date on contemporary knowledge, he would read, for instance, thinkers such as Descartes, Kant, Nietzche and others (1985:18).

Besides reading the thinkers, we need of course to be increasingly aware of the findings of other sciences and approaches that evolve with growing speed. Those findings and discoveries almost invariably point to the importance of context and freedom. For instance, as in the recent book by American psychologist Edward L. Deci. His courageous and incisive experiments about the different effects of extrinsic and intrinsic motivation are a challenge to the classic authoritarian thinking on the subject (Deci 1996).

Today (2001), the works of Maturana, Varela and his followers/associates are most up-to-date, accessible and understandable sources of our notion of the Human Being's essence and its functioning and, as a consequence, of how it is possible or impossible to reach the core of this slippery, well-defended and independent entity.

Furthermore, as it is an extremely rich and attractive view of the human being and the world, our point of view has spread very fast and in a somewhat disorderly way through enthusiastic (and often brilliant) but more or less hasty adepts. These were only superficially converted to that view and therefore were not profound. Those adepts could be found in all fields of culture and nowadays they bear countless names and faces, some of them very deformed. That is yet another factor that makes it very difficult or even prevents the comprehension of the essence of the view.

The attitude before that view and the discoveries that give support to it are paradoxical. On the one hand, it encourages specialists in the study, possibilities and difficulties of intervention in interactions because it gives them greater power (if most problems arise out of interactions — as for instance the therapeutic relation — the latter can also create conditions to "let loose" inner process in the former). On the other hand, there is fear and denial before the increase in responsibility (because of the awareness that we are makers of our history) that this added power could bring with it. Of course, there are also the natural fears and avoidance of coming into touch with the history of our interactions and the problems caused by them in us. Do not forget that we really are makers of our history but not as we rationally want.

For our use and protection against the labyrinths in which we can enter, we avoid making out in detail the multiple faces presented by that point of view (for, if done with competence and depth, it could perhaps take up the rest of our lives). With this self-protecting attitude, we try to draw from that global movement what is essential and interests us more closely as we leave the detail to specialists. I mean, the philosophers.

Undeniably, the great mark of that "novelty" that interests us deeply is the **recovery** both of the subjectivism denied by objectivism and of the objectivism denied by subjectivism. That recovery has naturally compelled us to favor increasingly the interaction. Putting the interaction into context is ever more indispensable for understanding the human being and his problems. The difficulty is that our interactions began too early for us to have a memory of them. Besides, we avoid that memory because it is often traumatic and painful. For instance, if we consider that those interactions began in the intra-uterine life (Verny 1989), then we can imagine the difficulties posed by the problem. To make matters even more complicated, if we consider the very plausible possibility that somehow there was and is relaying of experiences throughout the history of humankind and even before that, in the history of our pre-human ancestors, then we will indeed feel the absolute need to develop the indispensable modesty and humility to face that pretentious and often arrogant profession of ours.

Such an understanding of the human being as outcome, as creative integration of processes and possible adjustments in his interactions has made us see matters in a relative light and review our concepts. Notably, it has made us see things less often in terms of black and white, Heaven and Hell. The "politics of certainty" has come to suffer successively greater defeats. Let us remember that Heizenberg has opened this path to us.

With that, as we already said, the substitution of the OR and for the AND has established itself. In today's therapies, this substitution, this holistic view of being, is fundamental for the theoretical foundations as well as for clinical work.

Through that recovery, truth has come to be seen as an outcome of the encounter. Being can only be thought **in interaction, in relation, in contact**. Of course, then that being can only be understood in its context; given that he is unthinkable without his environment and history, his past lived experiences, his dreams about the future. However, naturally, we only have access to those things in the present, in the here-and-now.

That paradigm is viscerally revolutionary because it affects not only our rational opinions but also our most deeply rooted values, our oldest irreducible prejudices and, principally, our illusion of safety and the consequent need of control and stability. That is why even today it triggers some times violent responses in almost all of us. Those responses can be so violent that we often "choose" not to notice it nor understand it in its essence, in spite of the incisive discoveries in its favor in all sciences and all fields.

Societies do not want and perhaps cannot take on those findings in their radicalness. We too do not want (or cannot). For that might make us uncomfortably co-responsible for a lot of suffering that we prefer to attribute to other people and causes. Our self-image could be affected or, as Alice Miller repeats so often, it could put us in touch with our own personal histories and possibly with a lot of repressed pain, what we avoid at all costs.

The first paradox we face in order to understand those concepts not only rationally but integrate and live them is that, according to the concepts themselves, we are social beings in interaction. We are, we repeat, the creative adjustment that we have made in those interactions. Through a series of adaptation mechanisms, we lost ourselves as the creators of those adjustments and came to be ruled by them without being aware of relinquishing our power. Therefore, we are the outcome and are dependent on those interactions and yet we need to keep and develop our own individuality, our own identity (logically, our differences) in those interactions.

Usually we have to adapt to less favorable, strange and even hostile contexts. How can it be different in a constraining, controlling society that insists on sameness and uniformization?

Perls et al. (1994) say in chapter IV: "The conflict between individual and society is a genuine one" and develop from that an incisive etiology of neurosis. Or rather an etiology of the adjustments we have been compelled to develop and that, in a given context, are creative or at least provisionally "healthy."

We are therefore inevitably beings-in-interaction: we grow, develop, make ourselves up and shape ourselves up in those interactions. We are the adjustments, the creative integration of our idiosyncrasies and personal identities in the confrontation with external forces and possibilities. As those interactions have never been peaceful or ideal in this proponent world of wars (in which we need to be accepted and loved), we use the full range of our perception, all our wisdom and our creativity in order to survive in the best way we can. In that way, we distort and alienate ourselves as far as it is necessary in the utmost limits of our identity in order to adapt in the best possible way to those interactional processes. We should remember that those adjustments, when they happen, are always creative and even "healthy," whether the environment in question is favorable or not. They are healthy because they were the best possible ones at that moment and in that context.

Biology of Cognition says that our development only is possible through the interplay between the conservation of our identity and the adaptation to new situations.

The environmental novelties **cannot determinate** anything within de-living systems. The system protects itself and obstructs the entering of novelties considered too dangerous for the continuity of its identity.

On the contrary, if the novelty is not considered so dangerous, it may have the "permission" to enter in the system and may loose in it an inner process of structural changes.

So the essence of self-creation, the liberty of self-production (autopoiesis) is preserved.

In our terms, the person keeps his freedom, his power of agent of his existence and destiny.

It has been in that environment of doubts and creative discoveries, that atmosphere of confrontation of the established, of profound reflections on all the culture of the time that came up the figures of the great philosophers, psychologists, psychiatrists, biologists, physicists and neurologists.

They have built the foundations of what we are trying to understand and do here.

References:

Amatuzzi, Mauro, Martins. *The Rescue of the True Speech: Psychotherapy's and Education's Philosophy.* Papirus Editora, Campinas,SP, Brazil.
Deci, Edward L. 1996. *Why We Do What We Do (Understanding Self-Motivation).* Penguin Books: NY.

Heidbreder, Edna. 1964. *"Psicologias del Siglo XX,"* *Chapter XII: in La Psicologia Fenomenológica:* Maurice Merleau-Ponti. Paidós, Buenos Aires, Argentina, 1964

Merleau-Ponty, Maurice. 1985. "Le Visible et le Invisible" Pessoa, Fernando — Obras em Prosa, Ed. Nova Aguillar. Rio de Janeiro, Brazil.

Merleau-Ponty, M. *Les Sciences de l'Homme et la Phénoménologie.* Centre de Documentation Universitaire, Paris, France.

Perls, F.S.; Hefferline, R.; Goodman, P. 1994. *Gestalt Therapy — Excitement and Growth in the Human Personality.* The Gestalt Journal Press: Gouldsboro, ME.

Rosenblatt, Dan. 1991. "An Interview with Laura Perls." *The Gestalt Journal,* V. XIV, # 1.

Verny, Thomas. *The Secret Life of the Child Before to Born.* Ed. C. J. Moreira,

Virgínia — "Person-Centered Therapy and Phenomenology" — in *Psicologia, Teoria e Pesquisa,* Universidade de Brasília, vol. 9, Nº 1, pp. 157/172

In live systems such as the interactional therapies it is even more imperative to always put everything into question (therapist included). The answers needed to attend to the imperatives of daily life are always partial and contextual.

CHAPTER II

The Quality of Our Interactionships and Their Consequences

Human beings and societies are mutually constructed and shaped in the interactions. Therefore, what we are and do has sense in our existential contexts, whether or not we have taken stock of our history and our motives.

This shaping development began a long time ago. It is thought that three million and eight hundred thousand years ago our ancestors "already lived in family groups" (Atlas, 1995, p.32 and Maturana and Varela, 1987). Therefore they were already living and developing the first interactions, the first social groups. That is, *they were shaping each other, ruled by the first and greatest of needs, the need to survive,* with the preservation of their identities and, of course, by the other needs that sprang from it and were ranked according to it.

All we can guess about those interactions is that they could not be easy-going, peaceful and harmonious. There were difficulties and scarcities of all kinds. One fought for almost everything: for dominance within the group, creating rivalry between members, and for the possession and consumption of food gathered. And, of course, everyone in the group fought against other groups, enemies and/or predators.

In such an unstable climate of insecurity and vulnerability, the first habits, preconceptions and prejudices were developed, as well as the first roles and the first beliefs about who we are, who is the other and what is this world we are in (those habits and prejudices were, of course, at the time, the best possible ones). For instance, the habit of defending those closer to us from those farther from us. The latter were less reliable, more unpredictable and almost always seen as at least potential enemies. The different, the new, could not be reliable because it was a possible threat to the precariously established order and also the precarious security of survival.

In this way, the first alliances and the first complicity already happened "against" somebody or something: a common enemy, a rival group, large animals or simply the other or the different. Until today there are no fundamental changes in this aspect: we are urged since very early to mistrust strangers or those who are different. Figures like Hitler, Nicolai Ceausescu and others have been of great help to mantain and feed this defensive and distrustful behavior.

The Quality of Our Interactionships and Their Consequences

So, harmony, when it exists, is made "against" something: "against" enemies that are considered to be greater or worse for us. History is full of examples of sheer solidarity between peoples during the great wars or before people in "disgrace."

In this environment of mistrust and constant struggle for immediate survival or for the best way of going on living, the human being forged himself, was forged and forged society, in the best possible way. He did it always within the great contextual limitations where some tried to form (or deform) others in their image and likeness, clearly in order to enhance their own security and safety.

This state of affairs, this way of interacting has not changed to this day, incredible as it may seem to the less attentive. A lot of attention is needed to notice this plot, in the first place because we have always lived within it (somebody has said that the fish does not notice the water). The other difficulty we face in order to notice that plot is its disguising. A kind of pressure exerts itself in an increasingly concealed and deceitful way. Disguises and lies are developed to keep the status quo of violence without facing the growing, but often hypocritical humanitarian values. The open and established violence such as massacres, wars, rapes, remain fully visible, as well as conflicts that apparently arise because somebody else supports a different soccer team or because of some other fickle reason. There are abuses of every kind and various instances of lack of respect. Less perceptible are the subtle and well camouflaged instances of violence

---

that are as destructive as other violence, particularly because they go unnoticed even by aggressors themselves (in this way, they get rid of their conscious guilt). That violence is unnoticed but felt by everybody and, therefore, it yields a vital influence on interactions.

Even inside the womb — until recently proclaimed as the stage for a paradisiacal and unproblematic interaction — there is constant struggle (Verni 1989, and José Raimundo Lippi, a psychiatrist from Belo Horizonte, Brazil, who, besides others, studies and concerns himself with that first interaction and its consequences).

With such personal and ancestral history, it is no wonder that we are beings that are mistrustful and defensive rather than beings that are inclined to trust and have faith in ourselves, in others and the world. In war, everybody is right to mistrust all. The saying that goes "em rio que tem piranha, o jacaré nada de costas" (in a river with piranhas, alligators swim on their backs) is a good metaphor for the climate of most of our interactions.

The harsh reality is that we are the result, the product and the producer of that kind of interactions. We develop; we make ourselves into beings that **are wisely ruled by the need to survive,** in this inevitable and incessant struggle, in this war without truce. Noticing this would turn us into bitter pessimists if we did not pay attention to the fact that this way of being and this view of the world has developed as the best possible way in certain kinds of context and unfavorable and difficult interactions. However, those contexts and interactions do not correspond to any human "nature," (see the ontology of the modern movement in biology of cognition) and they can be modified, even though it takes a lot of work and suffering. Suffering that we always avoid and with this behavior we keep the status quo. Another existential paradox: avoidance of suffering is healthy in a situation of emergency and very dangerous as a fixed, general attitude.

Perls et al. (1994) laid bare those conflicts and their consequences, especially in chapters IV, VIII and IX. Their view is, as we said, little optimistic at first sight. For the Pollyanna types, it is even pessimistic, for it is a view shorn of any temptation of utopian romanticism or hypocrisy, founded on a solid and unprejudiced way of analyzing reality.

In her second book, Alice Miller (1984a) tackles the issue of **manipulation and abuse during childhood.** Based on ex-amples, she uncovers her findings on the motives for slaughters, cruel dictatorships, and serial crimes and drug dependency.

Edward L. Deci (1996) **experimentally** proves the fallacy of values that are the true pillars of our society, like competition, reinforcement and punishment. That is, in the case of all values that have as foundation authoritarianism, the force of extrinsic motivation has socially and historically imposed those values to the loss of intrinsic motivation. This last is capable of bringing us to a productive and happy life. It only appears when there is "support for autonomy" (for freedom) in the environment.

The Biology of Cognition's findings nowadays points to the same direction.

It is important to emphasize that those philosophically correct ideas, though they were proven in clinical, educational and organizational experiments a long time ago, are also subject to verification through controlled experiments. Carl Rogers (1985) already acknowledged the value of that kind of experiment, when he pointed out that the main chapter of his book was exactly the one where his ideas were subjected to experimental proof.

The problem seems paradoxical because, in order to place ourselves in a position of "realistic optimism" in regard to the viability of a happier and productive human being, as well as to the possibilities of interference (therapy?) related to him, in order to improve the quality of his life through healthier interactions, it is vital that we do not deny (as is our habit) the harsh and apparently pessimistic reality of the facts of our history and our daily life. The naive/romantic denial of unpleasant facts can be pleasurable and even healthy, if conscious and passing.

However, it generates serious problems if we submerge in it as our existential attitude and, in particular, if we repress awareness of it, if we live it in the dimension of oblivion, as often happens: "forgotten without knowing itself to be forgotten," as Bornheim (1983) put it.

The Quality of Our Interactionships and Their Consequences

Very clearly, that human being, producer/product of constant struggle, CANNOT only be valued "from outside" by any guru on duty. No matter how wise we are with our psychologisms, sociologisms, anthropologisms or philosophisms, we are naive sorcery apprentices before wisdom that was born, forged and developed throughout the millennia under such vital circumstances.

And that wisdom points to the opposite direction to that of ready-made, whole truths. It points in the direction of the humble Socratic wisdom, of permanent interrogation and awareness of its own limitations.

In spite of the obviousness of all this, this (wise) result that we are, this peculiar way that we have developed in order to better survive, in order to "get around," is always the target of criticisms of the rational thinking of the context. We are forced to take on those criticisms (for reasons of self-preservation and lessening of conflict) as our own, at some point in our lives, usually very early.

We come to defend them as our internal organization, our survival adjustments that were always inadequate incorrect.

Lack of trust in our own rational arguments (of our spoken or secondary discourse, that Perls called discourse "about" or "aboutism"), in our excessive amounts of explanations and theories, is always a good antidote to our lack of vision. That is so because, more often than

---

we imagine, those arguments, explanations and theories can be inspired, dictated and established by our avoidance and defensiveness, our need to avoid our own suffering and external and internal conflicts.

However, in some way and on some level, the same wise man that has repressed himself, who has "absented himself from our daily life" in order to adapt better (without integration), *also knows that he has renounced.* The awareness of this renouncement has however also been repressed as a measure of economy and in order to lessens the pain of conflict. On the same level, he is also aware that he is a victim of prejudices and his freedom to grow without preestablished directions has diminished or even ceased and what he has that is most intimate, legitimate and precious has been alienated. (For a more thorough treatment of this crucial issue so as to help us understand more accurately our position in what concerns the etiology of neurosis, see Perls et al., 1994, chapter IV, as well as the more recent work by Alice Miller, especially 1997, 1984a and 1993).

Because of all that lack of nourishing ground, our poor sage is discredited by all and particularly by ourselves. He is caught in the crossfire of external and internal criticism. On top and because of that, he is exposed to all kinds of saviors, of "illuminated" gurus, generally people adapted without integration to some presupposition in fashion. So they are always ready to "save" us according to their pre-conceptions and set prejudices. Whenever one kind of savior, of illusionist dealing in shortcuts to wisdom and make believe, wears off and

---

demoralizes itself, there always come up other kinds under other, somewhat different guises and with a different discourse. However, they always put forward shortcuts to wisdom, easy solutions, manipulation, guidance, and a dark pedagogy. **That is, they always put forward superficial problem-solving and more individual self-conquest and self-denial and, of course, the abandonment of the faith and confidence in the wisdom developed individually in his own history and the wisdom inherit of our ancestors.** (I shall insist on the bibliography quoted in the preceding paragraph, adding to it another work by Alice Miller, 1984b, where she examined the issue of **manipulation in therapy**).

The worst consequence left by these negative experiences is that, with each disappointment with one of them, our internal sage, besides becoming weakened by that inter-action, also becomes more defensive, more mistrustful and less inclined to unveiling himself. This defensiveness is because such unveiling has become yet another occasion for disrespect, for careless guesses and ultimately for invasion of his intimacy (it may be felt as a direct threatening to the liberty of our inner structures). That may mean in addition humiliation, shame, or simply the feeling of discomfort and lack of adequacy before others and, above all, a feeling of loneliness for once again not being heard, let alone understood.

We open ourselves in order to be understood and in order to understand ourselves better. However, we are

---

almost always disconfirmed with either brutality or subtlety. Subtlety and pseudo-acceptance are worse because they disqualify our defenses, our "resistance" that we have conquered and developed with so much hardship and suffering.

The Quality of Our Interactionships and Their Consequences

References:

Atlas da História do Mundo — World's History Atlas — Folha de São Paulo\Times,1995

Bornheim, Gerd. *Introduction to Philosophize (The philosophical thinking in existential basis)*, Ed. Globo, Porto Alegre, RS, Brazil

Deci, Edward L. 1996. *Why We Do What We Do — Understanding Self-Motivation.* Penguin, NY.

Maturana R., Humberto and Varela, Francisco. 1995. "The Tree of Knowledge" — First edition Scherz Verlag, Berna, Munique and Viena (1987) — Brazilian edition, *Editorial Psy.*

Lippi, José Raimundo. 1993. "Your Majesty the Foetus" Interview: *O Estado de Minas,* September 9, 1993.

Miller, A. 1994. *The Drama of the Gifted Child.* Basic Books, NY.

Miller, A. 1983. *For Your Own Good* (Hidden cruelty in child-rearing and the roots of violence), Farrar-Strauss-Giroux, NY.

Miller, A. 1993. *Breaking Down the Wall of Silence* (The Liberating Experience of Facing Painful Truth — A Meridien Book, Penguin Press: NY.

Miller, A. 1984b. *Thou Shalt Not Be Aware (Society's Betrayal of the Child).* Farrar, Strauss & Giroux, NY.

Perls, F.S.; Hefferline, R.; Goodman, P. 1994. *Gestalt Therapy — Excitement and Growth in the Human Personality.* The Gestalt Journal Press: Gouldsboro, ME.

Rogers, C. *Freedom to Learn in our Decade.* Liberdade para Aprender em nossa Década, Artes Médicas, Porto Alegre,RS,Brasil Artes Médicas, Porto Alegre, RS, Brazil

Verny, Thomas. 1989. *The Secret Life of the Infant Before the Birth,* Ed. C.J. Salmi, SP, Brazil.

"There is a conflict between the society I need to create in order to be accepted and unconditionally loved within it, and the authoritarian and love-scarce society that is already there, created by others and imposed on me. The latter chokes me with its values and prejudices" (inspired by Perls et al., 1994, chapter VI)

CHAPTER III

How Our Being Had To Adjust, Organize and Develop Himself In Order To Survive In Such Generally Very Adverse Contexts

In this way, in order to survive and find his way, that being developed in the best possible way, made some times strange adjustments and, in conflict with his context, modified much more that part which he had the power to modify: himself. That is, he molded himself rather than having an impact on his environment. In other words, his liberty of self-creation shrunk to the minimum limit possible.

The inevitable happened: our sense of lack of value developed itself, our self-trust became sick. Increasingly, we lost touch with the most intimate part of ourselves and developed a myriad of social, stereotyped roles generally created from archaic preconceptions that are there in practically all of us, for all who can or is willing to see.

And the resulting intimate dissatisfaction feeds the process of alienation of everybody and consequently also of society. Besides, of course, it leads us to seek satisfaction in some form of power over others or, at the other extreme, to hand ourselves over to some kind of vice.

This is the main reason why we show ourselves as basically **unhappy, defensive and aggressive**, and, above all, **fearful.** Somehow, we are always ready to shun responsibility for ourselves, others and society. Rather, we look for a scapegoat, what leads to us becoming incapable of developing any non-partisan reflection even in lesser matters. When an issue touches us more closely, then sectarianism entirely takes over, making us really crippled even in our ability to perceive.

This is the result of our perpetual, great struggle for survival the best way we can in this ever-present battlefield that has been — and still consists of — our interactions. Within such circular hostility, we build a huge castle of cards of rules, lies and hypocrisy. We are (also in order to lessen our pain) only partially aware of it, in a fragmentary and almost always incongruous way.

The deeper we are immersed in that world, in this castle of rules, the more we need to ridicule others that threaten to unveil our "secrets." We do that criticizing them in every possible way, denouncing and particularly satirizing them. Those undesirable innovators, those "enemies" of the status quo, those challengers of established truths can and commonly do present themselves as scientists, philosophers and artists in general. They are the butts of many malicious jokes and disqualifying mockery. Jokes that we ourselves spread when we self-proclaim ourselves "realists" (the ecology of non-change has been put into motion in order to keep the *status quo*).

That being is alienated in that way, mainly from himself. He needs the "politics of certainty" (even if he already heard about Heizenberg and his principles) as much as every being needs air. Hence the need to create a great Treatise of Truths that "must" rule over everybody. It provides the base and justification for the fact that everyone always wants to control everybody else, starting with themselves.

Now I feel myself divided between two positions: if I go on describing ourselves without any finishing touches, we will all begin (myself first of all) to feel bad (as I do already) and, in this way, we will inevitably mobilize our defenses. And, of course, as we are defensive, we will not find out, we will not see anything except our old prejudices. On the other hand, if I give in to the impulse of softening the truth, we may fall into the policy of indiscriminate and premature forgiveness and oblivion, as exhaustively denounced by Alice Miller (1997 and 1993). Or else into "premature pacification," a concept that has been so well developed by Gestalt therapy (notably by Perls et al., 1997, chapter IV).

As I am concerned with those opposite dangers, I will try to describe how I see ourselves and the world, in my moments of relative lucidity and some freedom from those radically opposed positions. It is relevant to note that they are opposed more in appearance than in their effects, as both serve the same purpose, namely, blunting our reflection and doing away with our findings.

This "Being," thus protected, is, by dint of his resulting lack of confidence and faith in himself and others, in constant war or at least isolated (and protected) by his own powerful armors. He (we) has (have) been shaped/misshaped in a context where the following have been either present or omnipresent:

> – Great destructive wars (almost all of them senseless) that we all know. Those were generally founded on the hypocritical excuse that they were for the good of humanity or some God. The other — who generally was on the losing side and in this way lost his power and control over the media — is invariably presented as an updated version of Satan himself, the Demon, the impure that has resisted the self-declared purity of the winner;

> – the declared or silent war of all against all, the division of people between dominators and dominated, or "oppressors" and "oppressed" (Paulo Freire), or "top dogs" and "underdogs" (Fritz Perls), or "active" and

"passive," each one of them induced by his own fears and in possession of a number of increasingly powerful arms as war progresses;

– The war between the sexes that undermines practically all relations and that seems so far from its end, with its denial of the possibility of disarmed love (see Michael V. Miller 1995). And as war is war, in this war, as in others, anything goes, even appalling practices such as cutting away girls' clitorises (today 74 million women live without their clitorises — Alice Miller 1993:75);

– The not less destructive inner conflicts (wars), brought about by resignations and the alienation of parts of ourselves, an issue that has been well studied by all the modern psychotherapeutic literature.

Most of those wars have been often denounced. However, we still resist those denouncements when they are sharper and more serious and, in particular, when they are closer to us, for instance, in what concern child abuse. In spite of being a fact that was first denounced long ago, it is only today that the press discloses the fact that it is parents or close relatives who are responsible for the largest number of cases of abuse. It is clear that society does not want to see, much less take on such truth. Why? Is it because it touches us very closely?

Alice Miller's studies and research say so. I believe that when we are able to really read and listen to that author, the directions of psychology, psychotherapy and pedagogy will suffer radical change, what will obviously affect all of society. The fact that her first book, *The Drama of the Gifted Child*, has already sold more than half a million copies (1997) worldwide gives us some well founded hope, even if it is hope for a more distant future.

By the way, hope is something that we do not lack in what concerns a future that is not, I hope, so far away. Hope that does not fade away even in the face of astonishing facts such as the latest discovery of neurology (1997) that child abuse can lead to brain lesions that remain in the adult brain. By the way, Biology, especially Neurobiology, is the science that is bringing to us the renewal of this hope (see the works from Humberto Maturana, Francisco Varela and from Biology of Cognition in general). That confirms the seriousness for all of society of the problem of violence in childhood, even in the physical realm. This fact will, I hope, scare us enough to make us cease to lessen the effects of that practice or disregard it. **Therefore, the human being, within the current contexts, has to be defensive and mistrustful because he notices more or less clearly that he needs to protect himself.** That which he knows gives him some confidence (an apparent paradox: the worse the context, the more he is attached to it because he trusts himself less to experience that which is different. **The context has not allowed him to develop the necessary self-confidence and self-esteem. In this way, he needs "certainties" and that precarious**

**security, uncomfortable and even cruel, no matter
how absurd they may seem to those that have managed to raise their heads above the "palisade").**

However, no matter how alienated and adapted without
integration, in some way and on some occasion we also
know that we have renounced.

Some important theoreticians (first of all Reich) tell us
that the more such renunciation lives on in the dimension of oblivion (we choose to forget it in order to survive), the greater the possibility that energy repressed in
that way will come up and manifest itself under the
guise of illnesses of all kinds. Another terrible solution,
but one that gives us more concrete and realistic clues
to deal with the problem and dream with its solution.

**The first cheering, more obvious and clearer fact to
be considered, is that all those illnesses do not correspond to any human "nature,"** to any fundamental
need: they are contextual illnesses. They have developed
and still are developing in those stepmotherly interactions that are (and apparently have for a long time been)
there. Therefore, they may not happen, or they may be
even altered, healed, if those interactions are substantially modified.

The dream is fed by the growing denunciations, made
possible by democratic (though somewhat shaky) re-
gimes that have been gaining ground particularly in the

Third World. In this way, such denunciations have ceased to be the purview of specialized works or of the First World. I shall quote as an example, among many other published ones, the article "A Carícia que Destrói a Inocência (pais, juízes e psicólogos começam a encarar a tragédia do Abuso Sexual de Crianças)" ("The Caress that Destroys Innocence — parents, judges and psychologists begin to face the tragedy of child abuse") (Veja, year 29, 5, March 31, 1996, pp. 76-82). Denunciations that are signs that the monolithic barriers of denial and the resulting silence are beginning to crack in a significant way.

Apparently all this is feeding a growing number of people who are more sensitive to the human predicament. All cultural expressions tell us that such people have always existed in small numbers, but everything points to the fact that they are more and more numerous.

Those people **have the time and energy** to think the human problems and those of nature, differently from those that only have them in order to defend themselves, make money, rise up in society and rule at any cost.

Carl Rogers has noted the growing numbers of those people as well as described their characteristics at two points in his work: in chapter XI in Rogers and Rosemberg 1977 and in chapter 12 in Rogers 1978a).

How Our Being Had to Adjust, Organize and Develop
Himself in Order to Survive

References:

Miller, A. 1993. *Breaking Down the Wall of Silence.* (The
    Liberating Experience of Facing Painful Truth) A
    Meridien Book, Penguin Press: NY.
Miller, A. 1994. *The Drama of the Gifted Child.* Basic
    Books, NY.
Miller, M.V. 1993. *Intimate Terrorism* Norton Professional
    Books, NY. (*A Deterioração da Vida Erótica*), Ed.
    Francisco Alves, 1995
Perls, F.S.; Hefferline, R.; Goodman, P. 1994. *Gestalt
    Therapy — Excitement and Growth in the Human
    Personality.* The Gestalt Journal Press: Goulds-
    boro, ME.
Perls, F. S. 1992. *In and Out the Garbage Pail.* The Ges-
    talt Journal Press: Gouldsboro, ME.
Rogers, Carl & Rosemberg, Raquel. 1977. *A Pessoa como
    Centro.* EPU — EDUSP. (only in portugueses)
Rogers, Carl. 1977. *Carl Rogers on Personal Power.*

Tension, censorship, auditory selection, etc are demands from the perspective of survival . . . (Perls et al. 1997, Chapter VI)

CHAPTER IV

Sense and Importance of the Concept of Resistance

The respect that we have for the so-called resistance and/or defenses is a logical result of the respect we have for human functioning such as it presents itself and not as it "should" present itself. That is in the essence and intention of our approaches.

Again, how has our being adjusted, organized and developed himself in order to survive in the best possible way within those often adverse circumstances?

> What is that being forged in that way? How does he present himself? How does he work? How he perceives himself, the others and the World? Ultimately, how he perceives?

> How has he adjusted his fears, scares or petty disappointments?

> Has he become, for the sake of self-protection, a shy and insecure being or someone manifestly violent or closeted?

HUMAN EXISTENCE

It is very clear and easy to observe that one of our most characteristic traits is lack of belief, lack of faith in ourselves and, hence, in others and the world. This trait answers for our need to control, to defend ourselves, to resist and, not paradoxically, to present ourselves as hopelessly grandiose people. Would that be one of the justifying reasons for the taste for despotism that is so rooted in our culture? There is also the need to avenge ourselves of the abuse we suffered mostly in our first infancy (see Alice Miller's analyses about the etiology of the behavior of mass murderers such as Hitler and Ceauscescu — 1984a, 1993).

All this is so because the context where we were shaped does not leave us many options: we need to set up or improve (develop) that indispensable resistance. We would be too exposed if we did not develop them. However, it is obvious that in this way our self-esteem and self-confidence, instead of growing, as would be desirable, through a process of unimpeded and non-deflected (self-sustained) growth, have instead become even more shaken. That is because we blame ourselves for the failures of our primordial interactions with our parents or our first caretakers and, afterwards, with other people. Obviously, all of them, in order to protect themselves and deny their own illnesses, blame us too.

We feel and actually become divided beings because of having suffered such process of alienation and denial of aspects of ourselves when these came to confront (or confront) that which the context wishes and requires that we be. That process touches us not only through plain imposition but also, mainly, by imposing its values and beliefs on us at a very early age, when we were still unarmed against that invasion. **In this way, we have abandoned ourselves in order not to run the risk of being abandoned by those people who were important to our survival.** We have developed a way of existence where our needs and longings give place to calls from outside; a system of behavior forms, roles, essentially geared to corresponding to someone else's expectations.

Thus, we have abandoned and lost touch with our intrinsic motivation and with our inner milenar wisdom. We have come to be ruled by extrinsic motivation. This last is endemic in our cultures. (On intrinsic and extrinsic motivation see the experiments in Edward E. Deci 1996).

This alienation, this renouncement makes sense because we were (are?) at the mercy of, unarmed and defenseless against the powerful. These take advantage again and again of our dependence in order to avenge themselves of their own sufferings and alienation. As they increase their power, they lessen the chances that they will feel inferior. The oppressor needs to maintain the oppressed in his role because the former fears an inversion of roles. Unfortunately, in this war, the oppressed does not only want to liberate himself, but exchange roles with the oppressor and, in this way, keep the relation oppressor/oppressed intact. This is one of the main concepts of the Brazilian educator, Paulo Freire.

It is vital that we remember with insistence that such process, the development of those abilities, roles and attitudes, initiated by our ancestors begins its development very early in ourselves. Too early for us to become aware of it, defend ourselves against it or resist in some other, less painful, less alienating and therefore healthier way for everybody concerned.

This division (in which what is truly ours remains at the bottom, without permission to come to the surface) alienates and deprives us, separating us from our most legitimate longings. For this reason, truly clinical work can only be one that creates conditions in order to facilitate the development (recovery?) of individual ability for creative integration (and reintegration) of those alienated parts, making us stronger and more in contact with our wisdom of beings who have in their nature the capacity for self-creation and self-realization.

However, that integration can only be realized at the same time as careful work towards reaching (recovering) a state of self-confidence and self-esteem that allows us to notice the flux of significant stimuli from the environment and develop the skills to respond creatively to them.

Resistance helps and protects us, but it also blocks our development and alienates us.

In order to deal with a minimum of competence with this difficult and apparent paradox, we need to pay attention to the obviousness of the issue: **If we lose that**

**self-confidence and that self-esteem in certain types
of interaction already exhaustively mentioned and
denounced by practically all the modern literature on
psychotherapy, we will only be able to recover and
develop them in interactions whose features are the
opposite of those that have disconfirmed and dis-
qualified us.** What is seen as diminishing or even loose
of power by whose that are in power.

Here lies the greatest virtue of the intention of our
psychotherapies and the greatest difficulty in understanding the radicalness of that intention and proposal.
The several kinds of resistance and defenses that they
prompt in us have so far not allowed for their full understanding. That is because society and, of course, the
professional community also need to defend themselves
from those novelties that their conservatism sees as
threatening because both are subject to the same laws
of self-preservation and survival that rule individual
behavior.

Maybe the old scientific habit of trying to be an external
neutral observer adds a few more difficulties in the
process of understanding this matter in which we are
inevitably involved emotionally, either we are aware or
not of this involvement (see Varela and Shear, 2000).

Do the roots of the genuine character of the conflict
between individual and society mentioned by Perls et al.
(1994) find themselves there? And also the roots of the
difficulty of the full implementation of that revolutionary

posture, that inversion of the way of facing the human being and, consequently, our profession?

We suffer cruel and systematic shelling from the beginning of our lives urging us to "mend" and "save"or "straighten" ourselves, very often through what is called a "good upbringing." On the one hand this shelling makes us believe less and less in ourselves and become increasingly dependant (what is after all what every authority and system want). On the other hand, it makes us develop at the same time, in a surreptitious and diligent way, our systems of resistance and defenses that are proportionate to the pressures suffered in the total context, both external and internal. The more we are cornered, the more we are judged, the more we defend ourselves, the more "resistant" we become.

In this way, this lack of confidence, of faith in myself, in the other and in the world has been a painful but absolutely necessary construction from the point of view of our survival, no matter how absurd, irrational and illogical it may seem when seen from outside — or seen only through reason, without regard to its meaning and importance in the unique existential context of each one of us where it has been carefully developed.

That simple observation, **no matter how obvious and noticeable**, incredibly is not yet part of the repertoire and practice of the vast majority of the teachers, health professionals and therapists of all lines and persuasions, even those that maintain they believe in it, such as

Sense and Importance of the Concept of Resistance

---

ourselves. As we set to work, our attitudes point the other way, the way of saviors, menders, manipulators, of the adepts of "dark pedagogy," of adjusters, defenders of the virtues of the cane. Those attitudes, we should stress, are obviously supported by lack of faith in the inner sage inside each one, including the inner sage of the one who gave to himself the role of therapist.

We seldom see therapists, in spite of the theory that they claim to have embraced, respect the resistance of their clients, their trainees or themselves.

However, the essence and intention of our philosophy and scientific beliefs clearly point in the direction of respect for those defenses. These were built through hard labor and they do not warrant fighting against them. They recommend that we should work with them, never against them.

In sum, it seems that genuine conflict between individual and society mentioned by all the modern literature on psychotherapy **generates** and is the **result** of an extremely old and interminable series of wars: war in society, war in the family, war between the sexes, and the worst of all: the inner war or wars.

Those inner conflicts (wars) logically begin in the process of adaptation, where society did everything to make us fit. A part of us ends up joining (it becomes society). It develops the idea that, in some way or on some level, we are wrong. This alienated and non-integrated part of

---

ourselves allies itself to society and its purpose of re-pressing the other part. This last is the part of our affects (love, hatred, sex and sorrow, in particular). The stronger this adapted part, the more we judge our own longings as inadequate and blame ourselves for them. That leads us to deny them with all our power. Fortu-nately this task is only superficially possible.

I believe that the difficulty I have felt in writing the last sentence is the result of trying to write it from "inside" the conflict: which is the part that is speaking, and which is the part that is now subjugated and alienated? And is that part full of resentment and therefore sabo-taging because it has been vanquished?

The near totality of therapies or therapists, in the best of cases, helps change some values, "updates" some stan-dards, but keeps the essential attitude: disrespect, disqualification and the fighting of "resistance." They do everything to impose their standard, their prejudice of what health should be, of what is right or wrong; dis-qualifying what has been repressed **(subject that voice-lessly keeps as an important part of us, influencing us on all levels).** The client easily follows the profes-sional and his prejudice because he has already devel-oped the roots of lack of belief in himself, fed by belief in authorities and, of course, in the "white cloaks." He is already used to not believing his own perceptions and feelings: he has since long lost Faith, the contact with his own wisdom and consequently with the habit to question and question himself, what made him a hostage of the "professionals answerers," So his self-confidence

and self-esteem. Alienation is crafted through constant
"experiences."

The client also believes that he must be "fixed," at least
in some aspect; in other aspects, he stoically resists this
attempted process of deformation. This last is a basic
belief of our culture as exemplified in the popular saying:
de pequenino é que se torce o pepino ("the cucumber
is molded when it is still small"). This saying points to
the deep-rooted character of that prejudice in our culture (and perhaps also in all other cultures?).

**The discrepancy between the discourse of therapies
and therapists and their action is proof that our
rational opinions only work in our discourse.** As for
our attitudes and behavior, these are ruled by our most
profound beliefs (Ribeiro, 1989) and, of course, by our
personal problems, prejudices and neuroses. These are
all deeply rooted because they have begun to take root in
(to invade?) in our personality too early for us to be able
to challenge them. Until very recently we used to say
that values begun to be transmitted through our mother's milk. Today, we know that the process of their
installation begun much earlier in our ontogeny without
mentioning the genetically inherited ones. (Phylogeny)

Avoidance and denial by many specialists (even though
understandable because of everything we have said here
about resistance inspired in the readings of Alice Miller's
work, notably her first,1997, and last books, 1993) can
slow down the comprehension of the roots of violence

and, therefore, of the etiology of resistance and distur-
bances. Without it, the development of better ways to
deal with the human being (psychotherapy, for example)
is often limited to the development of new roles that can
be more functional at the time but are as alienating as
the old ones brought by the client.

From this perspective it becomes very clear that our
resistance and defenses, painfully developed by us in
those confrontations that have been our interactions,
cannot be attacked, let alone dissolved. The texts do
not tire of saying that resistance cannot be attacked
because it often is the best way of survival that person
has found and developed. Therefore, there is a lot of
energy invested in it. What is to be done, then?

It seems clear that an important clue is to be attentive to
radicalness and obey, for instance, the main ontological
formulation of Gestalt therapy as expressed and encap-
sulated in the following statement: *"the basic law of life
is self-preservation and growth"* (Perls et al., 1995, chapter IV, 5).

If we take that formulation seriously, we find one of the
main (or the main) roots of the contradiction between
therapeutic theory and practice. This contradiction has
been challenging professionals for decades. It seems that
some of our masters, as for instance Fritz Perls, became
fascinated by "growing" and did not want (or could not)
see, as in Fritz's famous demonstrations, that **self-preservation is prior to and a condition of growth**. It is
not only growth's other pole, as he insisted so often. This

---

anteriority gives it a more crucial role by its closeness to the first of all needs, the need to survive, which is the basis for and supports all other needs. The hierarchy of needs (Maslow) cannot be neglected here.

That does not do away with the finding that the two needs of Gestalt's formulation support and strengthen each other. On the contrary, the more we self-preserve, the closer we are to our inner wisdom and so the greater the peace we have to develop our self-esteem and self-confidence. These are an indispensable foundations to experience the new and to grow (by actualizing potentialities and increasing skills). That in turn gives us more self-confidence and so forth. This is the unique way to develop a cybernetic really favorable to a happier and effective growth.

The problem is: what kind of support do we need in our interactions in order to have the basic confidence, the courage to initiate (reinitiate) the process of growth on our own and at our own risk, without giving up our self-preservation? This has to be set in motion without it being the result of a push by some visionary.

Even if that worked at first (like the "kick in the ass" in Herzberg 1968), it would awaken and develop our resistance and defenses, our protective system.

Without self-preservation there can be, and usually there is, growth of roles, of behavior desired by the context, by our rational knowledge or by the desire of our parents,

---

teachers or therapists, but not the desired integrated development of the individual and the unique aspects belonging to every one.

In order to understand better the dissonance between theory and practice in our psychotherapies, we need to go back to the pre-origins and origins of that dissonance. Our aim is to elucidate and understand a little better where *we have been captured by the classic prejudices of our culture* and how and when the deviation and distortions in therapeutic practice have happened. These last happen mainly because of haste and the functionalist urgency applied to overcoming a theory that has not been well digested and assimilated into practice. This last therefore becomes inevitably superficial, contradictory and often inefficacious.

It is not too much to insist that more or less hasty overcoming is inevitable, as the urgency of doing things imposes it. The client is there and cannot wait. The concern here is with the lack of further reflection, with the fixation of "truths" that are pre-established exactly because they are not doubted; with not examining whether we are distorting or not the purpose of our work, a purpose contained in our own roots. If there are distortions, what are their roots, our superficial grasp of theory, our prejudices, our personal problems or our fear of facing our own history, as Alice Miller insists so often?

What I am doing here is, to copy thinkers such as Merleau-Ponty, to insist that we should put everything into question, we should be permanent inquirers.

Sense and Importance of the Concept of Resistance

References:

Deci, Edward L. 1996. *Why We Do What We Do — Understanding Self-Motivation.* Penguin Press, NY.

Herzberg, Frederick. 1968. "Una Vez Más: Como Motivar a sus Empleados?" *Harvard Business Review.*

Miller, A. 1993. *Breaking Down the Wall of Silence* (The Liberating Experience of Facing Painful Truth) A Meridien Book, Penguin Press: NY.

Miller, A. 1994. *The Drama of the Gifted Child.* Basic Books, NY.

Perls, F.S.; Hefferline, R.; Goodman, P. 1994. *Gestalt Therapy — Excitement and Growth in the Human Personality.* The Gestalt Journal Press: Gouldsboro, ME.

Varela, F., & Shear, J. 2000. *The View From Within (First Person Approaches to the Study of Consciousness),* Imprint Academic.

"The problem of psychotherapy is to enlist the patient's power of creative adjustment without forcing him into the stereotype of the therapist's scientific conception."(Perls et al. 1994, chapter IV, 7).

CHAPTER V

Healing: What is That?

Every concept of therapy brings with it a proposal for healing based on the premises of what health or disease is. Those premises are made from abstractions made on the basis of conceptions on what a human being is. Those conceptions in turn are built in consonance with a certain Theory of Being (Ontology). Grounded on our theoretical constructs, today increasingly confirmed by clinical experience and the most diverse sciences, we come to understand more radically and clearly our conception.

The concept of health we put forward can only be thought from the point of how a human being develops his innate potentialities in his interactions with the contexts where he lives.

Our findings point out in the directions of acceptance of our differences and the liberty to develop them.

So, our conception is radically opposed to control, manipulation or coercion, whose use only makes sense when we are prey to pessimism and immersed in disbelief in the potentialities of the Human Being. In short, in his wisdom philogenetically and ontogenetically developed. They represent authoritarian and simplistic ways out. Their shortcomings have been increasingly denounced by the most diverse sciences as well by following the outcome of our forms of therapy in the medium and long run. The authoritarianism of control is seductive, but its functionality, besides being precarious and worn out through time, later raises problems and leaves scars. The balance is therefore substantially negative. That is what experience has been trying to show us for a long time. Why do we resist so much noticing the evidence? Worse, why do we resist so much listening to those who have noticed it?

At the root of this apparent paradox is the problem of dissonance between rational opinion, on the one hand (this when we manage to make it clear), in contrast with cultural values and our deepest beliefs, on the other hand (W. Ribeiro 1987).

Besides, there are our personal problems and the resulting avoidance and denials of all of us, including those of us who are self-entitled therapists and/or specialists in particular interactions. It is necessary to insist that this is a new view, not because of its age, but because it is still different and revolutionary in relation to the daily life of all of us, where authoritarianism rules. As it is an approach against the grain, it is understandable that there should be great resistance to its implementation and that there should be distortions as one tries to understand it.

Once more we must hammer on this old issue: the kind of conception we have of the human being and the world strikes directly at the heart of institutionalized conceptions, with the kind of belief that has been inculcated in all of us, in all of our interactions.

The deepest beliefs and those most difficult to uproot are those that still live in us, act on us but have been forgotten. We are therefore not aware of them, either because they have been foisted on us very early or because we repress them in order to adapt to the world that is out there and so survive better. Maybe there is some other reason too. The important thing is to be aware that at some point we were made to swallow them in order not to run the risk of being rejected, of not being accepted and "loved," even if conditionally.

Did it happen very early? There is vast literature and research showing that the earlier those influences (the first days of life, for instance), the deeper and the more difficult (or even impossible) to eradicate the feelings, attitudes or behavior developed then. There are also studies and research on the influence that we suffered in the intrauterine interaction (Verni 1989; Lippi 1993).

Therefore, the set of problems with which we deal is deeply rooted not only because its range is wide but mainly because it came up very early. Therefore, it lives on in us in the dimension of oblivion for reasons of economy of pain or of survival.

We like to say, "I have been like that since my childhood," as if this was a definitive argument in favor of some determinism. However, more recent studies and research agree with phenomenology and point in the opposite direction: we are predominantly social beings that are made, formed and deformed in our interactions. And at the moment that we say "since my childhood" we are already "old" in this "formation/deformation" constructed in the interactions with anti-individual culture.

The kinds of interaction that deform us are abundantly documented in books, films, radio and TV programs, magazines, newspapers, etc. I believe that critical rational thinking on how our upbringing deforms has taken account of that in a brilliant way. The problem has been the deafness to those criticisms by those who are responsible for our education.

Throughout this small book I will try to dig up the roots of the forces that keep those deforming interactions, in spite of the evidence of the evil that they bring us.

If we acknowledge and accept this state of war in our way to understanding/dealing with the human being, a strong cultural component comes into play: the will, almost the compulsion to "solve problems." Grandiosity?

Healing: What Is That?

Megalomania? Low tolerances to frustrations? Being anxious to get rid of guilt . . . ? Or is it simply the neurosis of saviors that made us choose this profession? Or did we choose it because we are irredeemably hostages to the classic prejudices of our culture? Maybe a huge hotchpotch made up of all that with a bit of our old fear of coming in touch with our own sorrows and problems.

It is difficult to tell. However, we do observe that we are taken by the compulsion to "do," "guide," "solve," "save," "cure," and "teach." We do not notice, however, that, as we do that, we are stuck to the superficial level of a problem. **Worse, we take away a person's chance to find his own way or catch a glimpse of possible solutions, strengthen his own "researcher," his critical thought.** All that would inevitably raise his self-confidence and his self-esteem.

Perls has often told us that Gestalt therapy is not concerned with problems. However, besides not explaining well what he meant by it, in his famous demonstrations he focused almost exclusively on problems. Once again we come across the lack of tune between discourse and action, speech and action.

Unfortunately, what was most often taken from Perls were examples of "therapy," contained in his demonstrations. Here the dominant model is focusing on the problem and trying to solve it at any cost. This has become to a large extent the model for healing in Gestalt therapy (perhaps due to our being anxious to find "solutions" and, of course, also because of our lack of skill, as some

of our teachers have emphasized, it became "Gestalt and
. . . " For instance, as denounced by I. From, 1984 and
1994).

To solve the problem generally means to try to make
conscious the flow of awareness or the vital flow without
taking into account the etiology of the obstruction or the
meaning that this problem might have for the person. It
became the keynote of Gestalt activities when in fact "the
creative nature of the resistance and the way of working
with it is, I believe, one of the revolutionary aspects of
treatment in Gestalt therapy" (Rosenblatt & Laura Perls,
1991:16).

However, Perls himself also insisted that Gestalt therapy
aims at helping us come more and more into contact
with the sage we all have inside us. It has been this very
same sage who, faced with our environmental difficulties, has determined the ways we should follow and that
still rule us, no matter how grotesque we may seem if
seen from some outside standard or the most sophisti-
cated existing theories.

Outside standards are in no short supply. They are our
fate and the existential challenge that we constantly face
in our interactions: to adapt to them, even though this
may mean our alienation or to face them somehow and
follow our personal development with all the attendant
risks of that attitude.

**We then face a trap: We both need environmental
protection in order to survive just as we need growth**

to develop our abilities/potentialities and also to better survive. It is a paradox because those needs with astonishing frequency become polarized and antagonistic. On the one hand, environmental protection does everything in its power so that we do not grow (if we grew we would become less controllable and less predictable); on the other hand, there is the inner exhortation to grow (we know on some level that that would make us abler and happier).

The more we study this conflict, the more obvious it becomes that the exhortation to survive is our main motivation. It is the first need without which there is nothing else, not even ourselves. Of course, our inner sage knows it. For that reason, in the face of any perceived, discerned, felt or surmised threat, *we abandon ourselves;* we give in to pressure, manipulation, and emotional blackmail and *do what they want us to do.* We become the gifted child (Alice Miller 1997), the well-behaved child, and the "number one" child that everybody loves and wants.

That is the most widespread way of surviving, so widespread that we mistake it for some human "nature."

It is a powerful and efficient mechanism of adaptation to situations of emergency.

However, the environment, the context and therefore the reasons of the renouncement of our own things in order to be accepted endure indefinitely and, in this way, this mechanism perpetuates itself. There is no emergency any more. There is no more creativity. The world remains like that: we are accepted and "loved" (and, in this way, our survival is more or less guaranteed), if we agree, if we follow the what and how according to other people's prescriptions. The condition for this acceptance and "love" is obedience above all else and renouncing ourselves and what we love most. We should remember the biblical story of Abraham and Isaac. "Love" is between quotes because it is conditional love. Therefore, it is not love, as Alice Miller has pointed out so well in all her work. It is "love" that *requires evidence* of reciprocity, that *requires renouncement,* and ultimately "love" that *requires.*

This etiology of neurosis has already been developed in a masterful way in chapter IV in Perls et al. (1995), even though the original edition was published back in 1951!!

In order to guarantee survival in environments that only accept and love us conditionally, it is clear that we develop an astonishing ability to notice what is expected from us. A mere gesture or glance will suffice to make us shrink or swell (often that attitude of ours is the pride of the family). Most of those who have been most hurt, who have suffered the most, go further still. **They do not need any external sign from the other in order to correspond to his expectations.** It is enough that the other — for instance, the therapist — has some project concerning those people for them to somehow catch the "authority's" intention and start to enact it. For instance, the client in the kind of Gestalt denounced by From, mentioned above, begins to have great emotional outbursts, as we can witness particularly in groups. The client of some Jungian therapists brings "archetypal" dreams, etc.

We come to therapy with that attitude developed throughout our (personal and collective) history and our life before therapy. We are anxious to correspond to the expectations of the therapist, the group and even the therapist's pets. **It is our old sage who is working so that we will succeed in the new environment**. The apparent paradox is that the more we have suffered with previous alienation and **the more distant we are from ourselves, the more we therefore need acceptance and approval from the environment, the quicker we learn the new rules, the** more readily we keep and widen our alienation and self-denial and the more we adapt to the new imposed standards. These last may be suggested or merely wished by the therapist and/or the group that become as a result happy with our "recovery," consolidated by the acquisition of new behavior patterns and new roles valued in that context.

It is in this way that many people get married or divorce, that children leave the parental home, that jobs are given up, all in a somewhat bold, premature and hasty way, without any regard for our limitations and resistance. These are then considered to be only impediments, usually in what concerns the opinions and projects of the "therapist" or "saviors."

For us, this is the main risk posed by some ways of working, especially because they bring about prema-

ture adaptation, thus generating the aimed acceptance. That in turn brings with it a good dose of well being because of the feeling of belonging, of being seemingly loved, etc. There is a measure of social progress, something has been learned and interrelational skills have developed. But the renouncing being has been strengthened with a role system that is more and more developed and, obviously, he is ever more distant from his freedom to growth.

Can we call such new adaptations and renouncements healing? Was it not the development of new roles what has really happened? Getting further away from one's own individuality? Less and less contact with one's own longings, affects and needs? The person becomes so distant from himself that he loses touch with his will. He becomes the **Maria vai com as outras** of the popular phrase, that is, someone without will who does what others do. He becomes *Zelig,* as in Woody Allen's film of the same name. That is so because higher need, that of self-preservation (survival?) had to function. Why? Because somehow our sage has caught the contextual demand and answered it wisely. He followed the popular saying **"dos males, o menor,"** that is, he has chosen "the lesser evil."

In spite of the frequent emphasis on the fact that it is not the aim of any psychotherapy, "conflict elimination" is exactly what the great majority of psychotherapists do. If we have some phobia or "weakness," some resistance of any kind that seems to bother us, the therapist hastens to use or apply a potent and creative technique to eliminate the "problem." Of course, that therapist is not to blame. We were brought up in a functionalist and pragmatic culture shot through with the neurosis of problem solving. How could we not have been affected?

On the basis of such findings the problem of what is healing becomes clear enough. The remaining problem is how to achieve it. It is a problem that is badly put, misdirected and not well digested. It seems that the anxiety to solve problems has kept us from the path of the therapeutic interaction and taken us to the other end: that of training (drilling), no matter how well disguised and subtly presented.

Maybe the same path that we have followed to make the problem of healing clearer is also useful to open a way towards achieving it. Constraint, control, manipulation and seduction as practiced in therapies, in a disguised way, whether or not the therapist notices it, are a very poignant example of what is not therapeutic.

We know that to do the opposite is almost impossible in an authoritarian world. A world that is judgmental, full of impositions and rules of behavior; a world that is therefore in conflict with our need of growth without preconceived parameters. We also know of the difficulties and dangers of confronting this violent and revengeful world.

It seems to us that the difficult attempt to find a way out should begin where we can, with some effort, yield some power: it should begin by ourselves. We become increasingly and constantly attentive to our authoritarian rancidity and the resulting defensiveness. Of course, we cannot do that without help, and help can only be found in interactions of acceptance, interactions that are really confirming. Sciences are becoming concerned with the necessity to consider the influence of the scientist/observer in the results of his experiments.

Many have already proposed an unarmed way of being with another (notably Barry Stevens and Rogers). What we are trying to emphasize is that the healthy, free and peaceful rebels such as Rogers or Barry Stevens do not abound. Almost all of us, made out of the human material that is at our disposition are still full of the rancidity, whether explicit or not, of authoritarianism and defensiveness. It is rancidity that commonly lives in us in the dimension of oblivion (we "had" to forget it in order to reconcile ourselves with the values of our "good manners," our "good upbringing" and ourselves).

For us, therefore, healing is not to solve problems but coming in conscious touch with the sage that everyone of us has inside himself (as Fritz Perls pointed out) and then do what that sage decides. Whether that means changing outwardly or not. He has always managed us in the best way he could and he is still managing us (for instance, he is shaping defenses/resistance), but we do not know it. Our ignorance of that is perhaps the primary cause of our not trusting the process and ourselves (is it possible that our sage works stealthily because he also does not trust us any more?). This ignorance leaves us at the mercy of all kinds of menders that fester in our cultures. I am very afraid of those menders that do not know that they are menders and deny it. They even honestly swear that they are only confirming and accepting us and never directing us, what gives them the necessary support to shape us at their will (they avoid checking with other professionals whether their attitude is right).

Therefore, **healing is the natural product that results from our Believing with a capital B in our sage.** Sage developed in our interactive experiences with others and with the World; experiences that begun in the intrauterine life and have continued to this day (ontogeny). They add to the wisdom that resulted of the accumulation of ours ancestors' experiences and the experiences of the ancestors of our ancestors (phylogeny).

Therefore, the biggest and oldest wisdom that we can imagine. In that way, what is **astonishing is not to Believe in ourselves, in our sage** and in our own capacities and, as a logical consequence, in the Other and in the World.

How can we do that?

References:

From, I. (1984): "Reflections on Gestalt Therapy After Thirty-two Years of Practice: A Requiem for Gestalt." *The Gestalt Journal,* Vol. VII, No. 1.

Lippi, José Raimundo. 1993. "Your Majesty the Foetus" Interview: *O Estado de Minas*, September 9, 1993.

Maturana R., Humberto and Varela, Francisco.1995. "The Tree of Knowledge" — First edition Scherz Verlag, Berna, Munique and Viena (1987) — Brazilian edition, *Editorial Psy.*

Miller, A. 1993. *Breaking Down the Wall of Silence* (The Liberating Experience of Facing Painful Truth — A Meridien Book, Penguin Press: NY.

Miller, A. 1994. *The Drama of the Gifted Child.* Basic Books, NY.

Perls, F.S.; Hefferline, R.; Goodman, P. 1994. *Gestalt Therapy — Excitement and Growth in the Human Personality.* The Gestalt Journal Press: Gouldsboro, ME.

Perls,L 1991. In Rosenblatt, Dan: "An Interview with Laura Perls" The Gestalt Journal, Vol. XIV, N. 1.

Ribeiro, Walter. 1993. "What We Believe In?" *Anales del V Congreso International de Gestalt*, Valenci, Spain.

Varela, F.,& Shear, J. 2000. *The View From Within (First Person Approaches to the Study of Consciousness)*, Imprint Academic,

Verny, Thomas. 1989. *The Secret Life of the Infant Before the Birth*, Ed. C.J. Salmi, SP, Brazil.

*The less "I am pushed" by others or
"push myself," the more I "walk."*

CHAPTER VI

The Non-Paradoxical Theory of Change

One of the classics of Gestalt therapy is the small but excellent text by Arnold Beisser,"The Paradoxical Theory of Change" (1973). It deals with the **clinical finding that the more we accept ourselves, the more we can change.** Beisser calls this paradoxical because it conflicts with our unexamined but deeply rooted belief (rooted in our culture and therefore in our psychotherapies) that we only change, grow or develop if we are tormented or apply to ourselves — or someone else applies to us — the law of the cane (or anything like punishment and/or reinforcement).

It is paradoxical because it conflicts with the basic and generalized lack of belief in the human being when he is free and accepted, as well as in our potentialities/skills. This lack of belief is cultivated as one of the important pillars of our so-called civilized culture. Maybe it is one of the classic prejudices whose eradication and even identification in our interactions is the most difficult.

This lack of belief goes so deep that it still rules even in the specialized circles of the human sciences. It is basically in opposition to it that rise the essence, proposal and intention of our view of the human being and how to deal with him.

Biology of Cognition came nowadays (2001) to give us a crucial help in the strengthening of this notion of human essence.

The theory and practice (when this last is conscious, well applied and coherent with the first) of our therapies radically give the lie to that lack of belief. They prove to us and convince us (if we manage to have the characterological readiness needed to let them do it) that truth is on the other side. Truth lies in the belief that the human being, in a favorable environment, inter-relating in a healthy way and not systematically suffering from pedagogical relations, develops his potential and changes (grows) without greater difficulties or traumas. **Or else he seemingly does not change**, if that is convenient and self protective for him, if that is better for his inter-actions at that given moment and context in which he lives.

If we are really accepted by people who are significant to us and if we accept ourselves, we stop judging ourselves and accepting other people's judgements. In this way, we develop (recover?), as a consequence, the self-confidence and self-esteem that are indispensable for the adventure of experiencing the new, for the adventure of living. And by experiencing the new in this way (lessening external and internal judgements and the resulting pressure) we become again freer and so we come to have the choice to keep on as we are, if that is better for us, or to change, if that change makes sense (and only then).

We can say then that that being has entered into his region of freedom. And that freedom is freedom: it is not freedom to do this and that, it is not freedom to change according to my rational wish and much less the "therapist's" wish or the wish of whoever it may be. There is no need to resist change nor defend oneself. For there is nothing to resist or defend against, as there are no pressures nor judgements, but self-confidence, self-esteem and the resulting peacefulness.

It is obvious that in this case essential change has happened, even if appearance denies it. The person has taken the reins of his living in his own hands. **He became (again?) the acting subject of his existence**. This gives him a feeling of power. It also gives him the peacefulness that inevitably modifies his being-in-the-world, even if his specific world, his existential context, requires that he play some role.

He will play it knowing that he plays it because it is necessary for his better contextual adjustment at that moment, without a feeling of guilt or inadequacy. These will have disappeared together with the feeling of worthlessness and lack of self-confidence that gave support to his insecurity.

Therefore, the person who accepts himself develops (finds again?) the degree of self-confidence and self-esteem that are the traits of a healthy being, independently from occasional crises or roles that he may have to play in order to survive better in unfavorable environments. And what is most important, he does it independently from the conflicting opinions of others about himself. That does not mean that he does not listen to others. On the contrary, he listens to others with the peacefulness and serenity of those who know what they want and need.

This is our simplest finding, also the most spectacular and important in essence, even though it is the least understood, least digested and, therefore, the least practiced in its radicalness.

Ultimately, it is reaching a state of self-confidence and self-esteem that are indispensable to our feeling in peace and in safety. That makes up the basic existential support we need in order to follow the flow of external and internal events that incessantly challenge us and that can destabilize us.

On the other side, what usually happens is that we remain within stereotyped ways of being and fixed patterns of behavior for insecurity and fear of not being able to deal with the new and the unstable. In that way, we do not accept ourselves because of the deep, old and well-rooted feeling of inadequacy for not being what we "should be." That is why we have to defend ourselves in some way. And, in order to defend ourselves, we close ourselves more and more to the world and ourselves and, obviously, to novelty. We become fixed on the old acquired patterns; we obstruct or deflect our interactive flow of development that is the result of the creative integration of continuity of our identity (self-preservation) and development (growth, adaptation). We become increasingly isolated beings, rigid and unchangeable.

Or else we play increasingly more roles, we alienate ourselves developing, without noticing, stereotyped ways of being that in the vast majority of cases has nothing to do with what we desired for ourselves in our innermost core. (See, for instance, the film *American Beauty*.)

This process that we were compelled to develop is so painful, because of the denial it contains, that, in order to lessen pain, at some point in our lives we decide to forget it. That is why it lives on in us in the dimension of oblivion, yielding powerful influence over us without us knowing it. This oblivion, like a powerful drug, soothes our pain and takes away our power.

The way this becomes rooted in us has been abundantly documented. See for instance chapter IV in Perls et al. (1995), the valuable books by Alice Miller (1997, 1993, 1984a), the new finds of Neurobiology (Maturana, Varela and others) and almost all the modern psychotherapeutic literature. This last has increasingly come to accept the importance and essentiality, especially of those first interactions, for our development and formation.

Beisser's theory is therefore very much correct. It has been clinically confirmed throughout the past years, but **it is not paradoxical. It ceases being paradoxical in order to become logical, as those studies, reflections and prolonged, accurate clinical observations elucidate further the process of conditions and possibilities of change as a process naturally resulting from the resolution of conflicts in favorable, non-judgmental and, particularly, non-coercive contexts.** The context we call the psychotherapeutic context is an example of such context, whose research and description make up our main aim.

References:

Beisser, Arnold. 1973. "The Paradoxical Theory of Change" in Fagan, Joen & Shepherd, Irma Lee, Eds. *Gestalt Therapy Now.* Harper & Row, NY. *Applications* — Zahar Editores — Rio de Janeiro, 1973

See also the references in the previous chapter and the references about Biology of Cognition in Bibliography.

Afirmar é enganar-se na porta. ("To state is to cheat oneself at the door") (Fernando Pessoa, Obras em Prosa, page 38)

CHAPTER VII

A Critique of the Instruments (Processes) Centered on *"Doing"*

Almost everything that has been done in the name of our phenomenological therapies is very far from the essence and intention of those approaches. On the contrary, it is closer to explicit or implicit authoritarianism, as can be easily noticed.

It is doing turned towards a more or less inconsequent seeming, with immediate aims of mere change of behavior and modified or replaced roles. These would be changed or alternated because they seem inadequate before some current standard or some kind of modishness. These are always more in consonance with the grandiosity of the gurus on duty than with the clients' needs. That, unfortunately, happens to all those that call themselves "modern" and that, for lack of consistent training, mix everything. The fact that they call themselves Gestalt, person-centered or dialogic therapists or make use of any of the innumerable existing labels changes little or nothing in the routine of seduction, manipulation and coercion.

Through our perspective we intend to get to an understanding of what we may call a favorable context, a different, individualized one. Context in which our identity, our differences and our individualized development will be respected. We understand it as a real context that is diametrically opposed to those responsible for neuroses, obstructions, and for the high degree of defenses and resistance that we had to develop to survive in the best possible way in those contexts.

This supportive, "psychotherapeutic," context that we chase after is necessary and indispensable for the creation of a climate propitious to integration rather than mere adaptation. It results from a interaction founded on mutual Faith and Trust that unfortunately is very seldom achieved.

Because it is a rare kind of interaction, we must often imagine it (as Galileo did with his non-existent free fall of bodies) in order to chase after it and in order to be able to conceive a parameter from which we can evaluate the degree to which we are going towards neurosis or psychosis in the interactions that we have. Of course, we also include those in our own interactions, especially those that we label "therapeutic." The evaluation of our own distortions is, even more obviously, much harder because of our denials and so it is practically impossible

A Critique of the Instruments (Processes) Centered on "Doing"

to carry it out without adequate help, hard work, wearisome reflection and persistence.

As many authors have already devoted their best efforts to describe the type or types of negative interactions, it becomes less difficult to evaluate the degree of deviation or interruption that each interaction brings with it, including (we should stress once more) those that "should" have been therapeutic.

We have only (only?) to begin to doubt, to constantly interrogate (see Merleau-Ponty, 1964, and Santin, Silvino, 1980) and reflect on some unexamined assumptions that are however at play in the interaction called therapeutic. In order to do that we have to face some classic prejudices, for instance, the one that says that the therapist knows himself, is healthier and wiser than the client is (see Varela and Shear, 2000).

From pre-conceptions flows naturally the pedagogic, autocratic shaping attitude that most therapists of any persuasion adopt. That attitude is nothing more than repetition of the classic prejudices of our society. Those prejudices rule the interactions of those who think more of themselves with those who are considered to be less than the former.

This has been one of the most often denounced attitudes in the work of all our teachers in all fields. One of the main aims of this book is to try to emphasize that the proposal of our psychotherapies is on the other side: the side of faith in the person's mechanism of adjustment, in his power of self-creation. Faith in the sage that everyone has inside him, whether or not they are in apparent contact with him. Now, to fully trust the human being is a radically democratic proposal. Thus, it makes sense to denounce radically also every attitude that points in the direction of control, manipulation, of dark pedagogy, by proposing the opposite attitude. This last is based on faith in the abilities and potentialities of the human being when he is free.

It is clear that the autocratic attitude has the support and encouragement of the old, deep-rooted, unexamined beliefs and prejudices mentioned above.

I insist that our cultures put their faith elsewhere, on the side of Authoritarian Thinking and its inevitable corollary: the multifaceted and ever-present ideology of the Cane.

As we turn our attention towards detecting the insidious action of these and other cultural pre-conceptions — that are inevitably part of us — let us reflect further on our "therapeutic" action and its congruence or lack of congruence.

Fritz Perls, for instance, insisted that Gestalt therapy is not interested in problems (but he also insistently took care of those in his demonstrations). Maybe because of that, or because of the eternal theoretical misunderstandings (or are they merely ignorance of theory?), we very often see Gestalt therapists struggling and trying to

A Critique of the Instruments (Processes) Centered on "Doing"

---

solve problems. They do so without the least awareness of what they are doing and no conscience that the aim of the therapy that they seek and claim to practice is not that. Problem-solving usually does the opposite of the aim of integration of alienated parts: it fulfills the grandiosity of the therapist and further develops the system of roles for both therapist and client, clearly weakening their inner power.

In that regard, Gestalt praxis has succumbed in the same way as the practices of the other therapies that have the same philosophy (maybe because of the same certainties and haste to solve problems). It has succumbed to the doer's attitude, the functionalist urgency, and problem-"solving," "saving" people. That is, it has become centered on what its own theory, its own deeper foundation calls "premature pacification of conflict" or the urge to "forgive" its aggressors, also prematurely. That is ultimately only adjustment, adaptation at all cost, succumbing to the oppressors' dearest longing.

What you often see is the therapist's doing almost exclusively imposing itself. His savior's urge does not allow him to give the indispensable support and time so that the client will develop his own capacity to solve his problems, what would strengthen his self-confidence and his self-esteem, the only reliable signs of health.

In our poignant work with polarities, for instance (that aims at the acceptance and integration of the alienated parts), it is common for the therapist to ally himself with

---

one of the poles of the conflict presented by the client. The former helps the latter to crush the pole that is judged and condemned (by both or by the therapist?) as inconvenient or inadequate. This is at least in part a complicity in choking or even murdering an often important part of that total being that came in search of help. This has been one of the most striking examples of lack of trust and lack of faith in the person's power of integration.

For instance, if the complaint or symptom is some specific fear, what we see most often is the therapist who suggests some "powerful or magical experiment" to overcome it. Or he enters into endless dialogues about the irrationality of that fear, etc, etc.

Disrespect for what has been conventionally called "resistance" is current. That shows a complete lack of understanding (due to characterological resistance or inadequate training?) of our theoretical foundations and behavior guided by the most deeply rooted beliefs in coercion, control and manipulation.

Why so much insistence in mending others and ourselves?

We believe that the cultural beliefs here have a deep rooted character of an unsuspected dimension. Alice Miller (1984a) has studied educational systems since the times of Solomon down to our days. She has concluded that *all* of those systems take the side of authority and

A Critique of the Instruments (Processes) Centered on "Doing"

the system at large to the detriment of the individual and his uniqueness.

The anthropologist Fernando Rosa Ribeiro has studied the roots and essence of racism in several cultures, particularly the Brazilian and South African ones. He has concluded that there is in our so-called civilized society a previous authoritarian flavor that is responsible for that and other classic prejudices (doctor's thesis, 1996).

Concerned about those perplexing research findings, clinical and/or empirical observations, we have proposed in Brasília to observe the incidence of that ancient flavor in ourselves as well as in our colleagues, students and clients. We have been impressed by the frequency of autocratic (high-handed) behavior in all of us in the least things. Most of the time, that behavior comes brilliantly disguised and/or covered up, for example, in the golden cloak of "best intentions," what of course makes pointing them out difficult or almost impossible.

Even though this may not serve as consolation, to answer the following question may lessen the discomfort caused by that finding: how can we be different inside this anti-democratic culture where we have been formed/deformed and that still surrounds us?

Scientists nowadays are very concerned with this bias (for instance, Varela and Shear, 2000).

Once more the characterological reasons for our difficulty in understanding our own radically democratic proposals become clear. And, of course, so do all the profound implications of this lack of understanding in our interactional attitudes, notably in that object of our concern: the so-called therapeutic relation. Even in the teaching of our philosophy and way of working we find still the culturally embedded autocratic tendencies. That obviously helps their perpetuation in our midst, as well as makes it difficult to actually understand the proposal. It also makes difficult the unveiling of the freedom contained in it that is its essence and intention.

As we are inevitably in a greater or lesser degree authoritarian, **and therefore defensive,** this way of being make us a bit deaf and dumb in regard to novelties.

Here too the statement in Perls et al. (1995) is pertinent: "fundamental mistakes are not mistakes of understanding but characterological ones." That is why it is useless and cruel to refute them. Therefore, it is very difficult to understand proposals that are so diametrically opposed to established systems such as the ones we embrace.

Besides lacking points of reference in that regard, we still have to face ever-present characterological resistance. Maybe we can find some sign of that attitude, the democratic atmosphere in opposition to the atmosphere of autocracy and laissez-faire (this last is usually dishonestly mistaken for a democratic atmosphere), in the old research works of Kurt Lewin. However, it is easy to notice in this authoritarian tendency the root of so much

A Critique of the Instruments (Processes) Centered on "Doing"

---

prejudice, the lack of faith in the Human Being's capacities, the pressing need to impose, of so much dark pedagogy, so much useless desire to directly modify myself and others. That is, the root of common violence, abuse and disrespect that we can witness everyday and, of course, of so much insecurity and defensiveness. Which obviously feed this negative circularity.

It is easy to point out the most obvious prejudices. The more worrisome are undoubtedly those that are the subtlest or those practiced in the name of Good. *For Your Own Good* is the name of Alice Miller's second book (1984a). It is precisely the book where Miller has devoted herself to the theme of the roots of violence.

The subtler prejudices are more worrying because in them those kinds of violence are difficult to detect because of their disguise. And, if due to some impulse of self-preservation we shun them, we become guilty because that self-protective action will certainly conflict with "truths" already solidly established in our way of being and so much the worse, will conflict with the projects of our dearest caretaker and with themselves.

Is to let go, to be authentic, to break loose, let it flow, to re-establish the vital flow at any cost, what we understand by growth? Is that what we propose as HEALING?

If that is so, then where to do it? In what context? Before whom? And, above all, how?

In most cases, this is proposed as if the client were an individual alone in the world, someone that lived in a cultural void and without prior education, as if he did not depend on his environment, as if he weren't a social being. Fritz has also contributed (in the demonstrations and in some of his writings) to this individualistic (isolationist) view of the human being. That would lead us to deny the being-in-interaction that is at the base of all our theory. Fortunately, Perls himself, in his courageous and elucidating *In and Out the Garbage Pail* and "A Life Chronology" (1993) has given us clear clues to his own deviations and problems and how they developed. These have influenced and even determined his way of acting. These also serve as an example for us to reframe the difficulty of fully adopting a way of being that is so deviant. **Maybe his example of taking into account and fearlessly disclosing his own wounds and problems will be one of his greatest legacies and, not without reason, one of the least followed or used.** To hide our problems, not to "do one's dirty linen in public," is another powerful classic prejudice of our mistrustful culture with its low level of self-esteem. However, this open attitude can also be, like many others, a disguise for our grandiosity.

The actual person before you has learned and inherited answers, developed and tested behavior patterns in specific contexts where everything makes sense. We therapists only have access to them through what that actual person tells us, and even then only in a precarious way. He tells about them or hides them from us consciously or not.

A Critique of the Instruments (Processes) Centered on "Doing"

That person had to choose to "forget" many things that still influence his behavior for many reasons. Because they were dysfunctional or uncomfortable, or because they brought along a lot of pain. He has adjusted in a particular, unique and creative way in order to survive better in the best possible way in his context.

Those adjustments, in some way, may have become or are in the process of becoming dysfunctional. That is why that person has looked for us (in case it was not because of sheer fashionableness or outside pressure). **However, with astonishing frequency, those old adjustments still make up the best way of surviving in his perceived context.** Other arrangements and other adjustments, no matter how wise they may seem to the therapist and the rational thinking of the client, usually destabilize the latter's existential ground. They heighten old conflicts and create new ones. Then the person can find himself in unbearable situations. For instance, I have seen again and again therapists who have facilitated and even forced the separation of couples, inspired in some problem framework that was exclusively logical.

I have observed the disastrous consequences through the years, of two cases of that type of "therapeutic intervention." It is clear to me that much suffering and waste of precious time could have been avoided if the therapists had been more modest and less arrogant and had only (only?) been poignantly present and supportive in order that the best possible solution at that point could be construted. A solution that could still be unknown to both client and therapist, or even non-existent at that moment.

What lacked is ever clearer: **there was a lack of faith in the potentialities and abilities of the clients. There lacked faith in the human being in general** and there was plenty of arrogance and pretentiousness (the actions we witnessed were not performed by beginners, on the contrary).

The person is divided, is in conflict.

Perls et al. (1995, chapters VIII and IX) have dealt in a magnificent way with the problem of conflict. Chapter IX was considered to be so good that it came out once more in the collected works of Paul Goodman (1977). The original edition of Perls et al. came out in 1951.

The situation is therefore much more delicate, complicated and bigger than can be gleaned from "outside," even if "outside" is the client's own rational perception.

For instance, the client may be in agonizing conflict.

At that moment, our worst enemy can be and generally is our tendency of being saviors, problem-solvers and, obviously, our resulting haste. **The person has lost faith in himself and we do not have enough faith or any faith at all to help him reassure himself and trust that a solution will certainly come if both have confidence in it.**

A Critique of the Instruments (Processes) Centered on "Doing"

I do not know anybody that has enough faith in the human being to reassure us at crucial points (maybe Rogers, Irma Lee Shepherd and Barry Stevens are the known exceptions that confirm the rule).

Try to think of a practical test for you and your friends and give yourselves a mark. I have never seen anybody, after accurate and honest self-examination, to obtain the highest mark in what concerns having faith in another or in himself. Is it possible that we would need to be born again, in another culture, with other parents, other educators, in order to achieve it? Is that pessimism or observation?

The assertion that we are the products of creative adjustments in circumstances that are both favorable and unfavorable is quite clear and widely accepted. Those were the adjustments that were possible in the context in which they happened. We have only partial knowledge about them. They were often developed with great effort and suffering. They are still functional and still make sense in our lives and therefore can only be actually noticed and tested in very special interactions of acceptance where our need to defend the continuity of our identities (survival) diminish (see Maturana and Varela works). Those interactions are therefore opposed to and deny the interactions where the adjustment happened. That adjustment may be considered to be inadequate today. Is it real inadequacy or is it judged to be so because it does not meet some external (more modern?) standard? These are some reflections about the difficulty of "therapeutic action." Other difficulties that I have been able to find out are pointed out throughout the book.

In general, we think that the great difficulty in our therapeutic action results from only one problem: the fact that we are more or less in dissonance, emotionally rather than intellectually, in relation to the democratic (in fact anarchist) essence of the psychotherapy we are trying to develop.

That is why we believe in the effort to make our action coherent with theory. I must insist that it is not easy because of the classic cultural prejudices that point the other way, the way of control, lack of freedom, fixation, the almost absolute belief (whether or not it is perceived) in the ready-made truths of our culture. It seems that Heizenberg's "uncertainty principle" does not affect (or infects?) the human sciences.

A culture that is in decay and about to collapse is perhaps, on account of that, as dangerous as a hurt animal. These cultural prejudices make it difficult or prevent us from trusting and accepting others and ourselves. Such acceptance and trust are the only possible way out, the only door that every authority, even that authority that has only itself to control, insists on keeping closed.

A Critique of the Instruments (Processes) Centered on "Doing"

References:

From, Isadore. 1984 & 1994. "A Reflection on Gestalt Therapy After Thirty Two Years of Practice. A Requiem for Gestalt." *The Gestalt Journal.*

Miller, M.V. 1995. "Introduction to the Gestalt Journal edition" - In Perls, F., Hefferline, R. & Goodman, P. *Gestalt Therapy: Excitement and Growth in the human Personality.* The Gestalt Journal Press: Gouldsboro, ME.

Miller, A. 1983. *For Your Own Good* (Hidden cruelty in child-rearing and the roots of violence), Farrar, Strauss, Giroux, NY.

Miller, A. 1993. *Breaking Down the Wall of Silence* (The Liberating Experience of Facing Painful Truth). A Meridien Book, Penguin Press: NY.

Ribeiro, Fernando Rosa. 1996. 'Apartheid' and Racial Democracy: South Africa and Brazil in Contrast" doctoral thesis. Utrecht, Holland.

Perls, F. S. 1992. *In and Out the Garbage Pail.* The Gestalt Journal Press: Gouldsboro, ME.

Perls, F. S. 1993. "A Life Chronology," *The Gestalt Journal.*

Perls, F. S.; Hefferline, R.; Goodman, P. 1994. *Gestalt Therapy: Excitement and Growth in the Human Personality.* The Gestalt Journal Press: Gouldsboro, ME.

Goodman, P. 1991. *Nature Heals (The Psychological Essays of Paul Goodman).* Taylor Stoehr (Ed.) The Gestalt Journal Press: Gouldsboro, ME.

Varela, F.,& Shear, J. 2000. *The View From Within (First Person Approaches to the Study of Consciousness)*, Imprint Academic.

Merleau-Ponty, Maurice. 1964. *Le Visible et l'Invisible*. Gallimard: Paris, France.

Santin, Silvino. 1980. 'Pensamento Caminho' (Thinking Path) ou 'Pensador Caminhante' (or Walker Thinker) — Um Perfil de Maurice Merleau-Ponty (A Maurice Merleau-Ponty Profile) (Revista do CCSH, Universidade de Santa Maria, RS, Brasil, pgs. 489/512.)

The "confirmation" of the person of the therapist, which happens so commonly in the therapeutic relation, only feeds his grandiosity whereas the client feels an increasing lack of confidence and worthlessness. In that way, it has a regressive effect on both of them.

CHAPTER VIII

What Should be Done?

In the first place, it is indispensable that the aims of "doing" should be clear and that those aims constantly pervade and give support to action. The main proposed aim is to concentrate on establishing an interaction that makes possible the re-establishment and/or strengthening of SELF-CONFIDENCE and SELF-ESTEEM, the only sure indicators of health.

It is only in that kind of interaction that we can actually break down barriers and enter with confidence into the dark alleys of our histories and ways of being or simply acquire the indispensable and healthy habit of turning to ourselves without defensiveness. It is a interaction where the other is only (only?) with us intensely present, without any project for our health or for us. His attitude is therefore non-judgmental, and one of positive, unconditional and empathetic consideration (Carl Rogers), of confirmation (Martin Buber), of belief in and support for the development of our creative integration.

That is, it is an attitude of belief in our individual and unique way of being (Gestalt therapy), of liberation of the oppressed and oppressor (Paulo Freire). It is also an attitude of true support for autonomy (Deci), and belief in our inner power and wisdom of self-creation and self-development.

The different ways of conceptualizing it point in the very same direction, the direction of the essence of the "therapeutic" attitude, of the proposal of all therapies that value above all the potentialities of the human being and his capacity inside interactions.

Those therapies believe that those qualities enable us to always choose and do what is best, when we are free and unhindered. It is the true and radical faith and confidence in the ancient inherited (phylogeny) and developed (ontogeny) wisdom of the human being.

The human being has to fully live and grow, which is at the core of phenomenology and of its method, now appears in biology with all its strength, splendor and scientific confirmation.

Breaking down barriers and avoidances is effective, lasting and without aftereffects because it has happened and happens without violence or coercion of any kind and chiefly because the breaking down happened by our direct intervention in liberty what made us grow as our own destiny makers.

It is a kind of interaction where our defenses, our neuroses, our endemic defensiveness are fully dispensable because they are useless: they have lost their functionality.

We start therefore from a theoretical observation (strongly empirically proved) that both neuroses and healing are the product of interactions. Therefore, both the former and the latter develop as responses to contexts and specific interactions.

Based on that we can only propose that the interaction said to be therapeutic be radically opposed to those that drove us away from our own strengths and wisdom. That means that a supportive, confirmatory, non-judgmental interactionship that does not bear pedagogical attitudes is absolutely necessary to approximate us to these strengths and wisdom.

The main difficulty in establishing that interaction is that almost all of us think we practice it, when in fact reality shows otherwise. Even those that cultivate and practice it do it sporadically only. What usually happens, as can be easily witnessed by any of us (if we are willing to), is the attempt to frame the client within our parameters, our beliefs and prejudices. It is clear that this happens due to our cultural formation/deformation, abundantly confirmed and implemented in practically all our interactions including our therapeutic apprenticeship.

The cultural belief that is profoundly rooted in us that we are children of original sin and/or that we bear some inevitable negative and dangerous tendency justifies the resulting belief that we need to be controlled and/or saved. It obviously does not allow us to believe in ourselves. We have to fix (save) others and ourselves. This can be one of the variables that have caused so much lack of belief in ourselves and so much belief in the miraculous effects of the cane: "if I let it run loose . . . "; "if we don't control this girl . . . "; "if I begin to cry, the world will be flooded"; "if I let my rage out, I will kill everybody." These are some of the examples of so many of our catastrophic expectations, all supported by the lack of confidence in the human being. They all lead to one purpose: justification through coercion in order to control, manipulate and shape.

The origins of this *lack of belief* can still be the subject of research, studies or theoretical speculations, but the fact of its existence is there and cannot be denied. And *as it is the ideological support for all violence*, we cannot discard or ignore it. It is clear that the process of violence, once initiated, goes on by itself, for instance, by the need for vengeance that it triggers (consciously or not, but it always re-feeds the process). However, even the violence clearly carried out in vengeance uses to bring as a justification the excuse of acting as a Good Samaritan to fix, improve and save. The Devil himself must say that he acts "for our own good."

What Should Be Done?

It says that it is comforting to enter in contact with the finds of modern biology, by which our nervous system works in a collaborative and solitary way. It once more teaches us that competition and defensiveness were and are cultural develop-ments.

Our interventionist neurosis does not allow us to have faith in the proved fact that if things flow without obstacles and pushes all will happen in the best possible way in that historical moment and that specific context. And the being will construct (develop) itself in that direction. We have almost no parameter in our culture that allows us to believe in this: it is a very rare moment when we are unconditionally accepted even and perhaps particularly within the existing psychotherapies.

Maybe Barry Stevens had this experience when, in 1918, she "left the school because . . . " (in *Person to Person — The Problem of Being Human* — Carl Rogers, Barry Stevens and others — Real People Press: 1967. She said that to introduce herself towards the end of the book: "About the Authors"). It's easy to imagine that she has had the indispensable family support to assume this courageous decision. Even today, more than eighty years after, I don't know families with that disposition and confidence.

That is the reason why we cannot guide our doing by following only our "spontaneity." Unfortunately, this last is not reliable. It would only be so if we showed a degree of health that we do not have. Imagine (or remember), for instance, the effects of the spontaneity of a grandiose person, a savior, a seducer, a manipulator or someone who flees suffering as the Devil flees the cross, of a closeted shy person, of a tyrannical fascist or a war tank.

Therefore, if we let our action run spontaneously, without critical reflection, very possibly our autocracy will take the reins of that doing. If you will be attentive and observe your surroundings and some times, why not?, yourself, you will see this happen.

Paulo Freire has defended the thesis of the mutual dependence of action and thought. He said (to a group of Gestalt therapists) that whoever exaggerates in action usually does things inconsequentially and that whoever exaggerates in thought generally becomes a mind-fucker. We therapists should yet add to that our personal problems that deviate and/or obstruct the answers of everyone. Here too we drove over our **"natural biologic impulse of altruism and collaboration"** (Maturana and Varela, 1987, p. 24). We also drove over the way our own brain functions as a **"system of very height cooperation"** (Varela, *"Connaître,"* page 58).

Violence (oppressiveness) is profoundly rooted in our culture and, therefore, in some way, it is part of ourselves. I do not believe it is necessary to give examples of that. I only (only?) ask you to be attentive to how much violence, trespassing, and disrespect you see and/or take part in everyday. The issue therefore seems to me not to be one of whether I am an autocrat, but in what measure I am one.

What Should Be Done?

Perceiving and accepting that fact is not so painful as could seem at first sight if we understand its inevitability for cultural and, logically, historical reasons. This frees us from the guilt of not being the "perfect beings that we should be," that all wanted and required us to be. Here too, once more, though painful, the acceptance is liberating.

The autocratic figure is a curious figure, full of ambiguities and conflicting polarities. For instance, exaggerated timidity can be a mask with which the grandiose despot shows himself; the exaggerated extrovert usually masks great timidity and so forth. Of course, one of those aspects of ours can be oppressing and/or denying the other.

All those masks are carefully developed defenses and they almost always still have their function and sense within the view of self and the world of the person that defends himself.

I believe that this need to deny parts of ours, oppressing them, is another of the factors we face that cause the most difficulty in order to understand radically the democratic (even anarchist) proposal of our human and therapeutic view. And, of course, when I say to understand radically I mean understanding that is not only rational, responsible for our intellectual opinions, but deeper acceptance on the level of affect, emotions and commitment. It is only this kind of understanding that is able to alter our beliefs and so our attitude before the other, the world and ourselves. It is therefore the only way to radically change our actions.

Gestalt Therapy's statement that "conflict between the individual and society is genuine" (Perls et al. 1995, chapter IV, 6) takes us to the heart of the matter and should be reflected upon and discussed as far as our limits (limitations) will allow it.

I like to insist on the point of "as far as we can." It is an undeniable truth, and one easy to observe that, especially in matters that involve and touch us such as this one, if we do not take into account our limitations, our neuroses, the neuroses and prejudices of our culture, we will remain only on the surface. Or we will avoid without noticing it the most crucial aspects of the issues under study. The statement by Perls and others (1995, chapter II, 6) that "fundamental errors are invariably characterological" and therefore "cannot be refuted" tells us about the cruel uselessness of trying to argue logically and scientifically against them.

And the present issue — the genuineness of the conflict between the individual and society — is consequently one of the greatest generators of conflict and therefore avoidance, rationalizations and development of alienating roles. It obviously makes difficult the full understanding of new approaches that favor the human capacities in liberty by opposition to the cultural beliefs like ours.

What Should Be Done?

We fear the conflict they bring because they are possibly destabilizing agents in our existential arrangements. This fear, we must insist, is genuine because it directly affects our existence, our self-image and often, our own survival. That is because it also has a destabilizing power over the total field in which we take part: our family, work environment and, why not, our own society.

I believe that being over-insistent on this matter is of the utmost importance because of what we have seen that all kinds of agents of change, notably "therapists" or psychological professionals in general, make with their victims. They destabilize the ground of our lives without the least care, and therefore in an irresponsible and even criminal way. How many clients have arrived at your office completely lost because of previous therapies? Or how many people have you destabilized yourself or at least shaken in the name of some therapeutic truth without measuring the possible consequences, or only precariously measuring them? Put in another way, how many times do we at least help people shake or even destroy the ground of their existence without their having had the time to build new ground? Have you ever helped or seen other professionals help clients to get a divorce or get away from their families prematurely or untimely? It is important that naming it "premature and untimely" is not due to judgment on the part of the therapist, but is a result of observation linked to the consequences of the separations on the short, medium and, if possible, long run.

What do we need in order to become more supportive without directiveness so that the people before us will not feel invaded or abandoned?

I believe in the following steps:

1 — To accept ourselves and our limitations;
2 — To develop (recover?) the indispensable Faith in the Human Being and, as an inevitable corollary, in his abilities and potentialities, when he is free and supported.

It is not too much to remind ourselves that the human being and his ancestors and the ancestors of these ancestors have developed their existential wisdom and ability to survive for millions (or billions if we add the accumulation of pre-human experiences) of years. **The origin of the sage we all have, mentioned by Perls, must be there, as well as the origin of so much caution, fear and defensiveness.** Our personal history is repressed and the history of humanity is too old, rich and complex for us to be fully aware of it. But our ignorance is only on the surface: our sage knows, and knows those histories and therefore always takes them into account.

I insist that in last decades the Biology of Cognition has greatly contributed to clarify this subject.

To believe fully in that inner sage inside each of us is our main means of really acquiring the indispensable conditions to give support to the other so that he will grow (or

---

not) according to his needs and possibilities and not according to our intentions, theories and/or anguish.

It is often said that in order to really understand our scientific/philosophical paradigm we have, rather than understanding it rationally, to convert ourselves to it.

If that is so, and everything points that way, what is our conversion like?

We believe that the simplest, most valid and easiest parameter to measure our conversion is to evaluate the extent of our **Faith in the Human Being.** And that is not so difficult to measure, especially if we do it with the help of other people who are also interested in their evaluation. Our enemy here is our grandiosity.

How and how much do I intervene? In my children's lives, in my home, in the life of my partner, in my work groups, in my studies? In the life of my clients? What kind of excuse do I have to interfere? What is my defensiveness like?

Let us make an experiment and imagine ourselves not intervening in those situations. Will the world end? Or will we find out that we are not that wise and irreplaceable? (Which is also dangerous, besides fear arousing).

A curious, important and non-paradoxical aspect of this research on the extent of our faith is that in it we also find out and measure the extent of our despotism: the more faith we have, the less despotism we show and vice versa.

The most important thing in this evaluation, however, is not to blame ourselves for the results, what would make us go back to the despotism against ourselves, falling back into the circularity of neurosis. Despotism is very old in spite of not being part of our essence or nature (see Biology of Cognition) and therefore must be ingrained in our flesh and bones (in our cellular memory?). Let us carry out our evaluation reminding ourselves of the precepts of our approach. It states that we **should not** and **do not have to** do anything about it, let alone nag or martyr ourselves. We have only (only?) to accept ourselves the way we are and leave the problem of creative integration to our old sage.

Is that not the key to our healing?

If we really accept ourselves, we will accept the other that will have in this way the indispensable support and the chance to accept himself too.

The inevitable corollary is a significant raise in real self-confidence and self-esteem, the only reliable signs of health and the only reliable instruments to evaluate our way of being in the world and know whether it is really doing us a service or a disservice.

What is to be done also seems paradoxical because it is in truth not doing rather than doing. Or at least it is to rein in our compulsion to do, to intervene, interpret and solve problems.

In order to have an idea of the extent of our historic prejudices that are responsible for our fears and defenses, I suggest that we remember the poetic/child-like image of the forest "where things had no name" (Lewis Carroll, 1994, pp. 43-45). I believe this can be one of the best examples of how to put ourselves between brackets according to the precepts of mathematician and philosopher Edmund Husserl and his phenomenological method. If these are indeed a good example we are very close to something we could really consider as an attitude, a therapeutic attitude. That is because we are at the intersection between the purest poetics of child literature and therefore of dream and the most rigorous form of scientific/philosophical thinking.

At this meeting point, a point of contact with the other through this unarmed way of being, this attitude without presuppositions, we can establish an interaction that is really non-judgmental and free from the load of prejudices that rules us and frees us from all the insidious dark pedagogy that has contaminated our interactions without us being in a condition to defend ourselves.

That is because those prejudices are mostly ingrained in ourselves and, what is worse, in the dimension of oblivion. Therefore they work automatically. We only notice their presence and dimensions when we go into the forest "where things had no name": in it, we will be the girl that can run freely and cheerfully with one arm around the little animal. However, as we go out, we will take on again the great load of beliefs, names and pre-conceived ideas and we will flee the situation. How can a girl spend time and travel with a small unknown deer? And how can a small deer be a companion and trust and travel so closely to a human being that it has just met?

That naked and decontaminated journey is the moment of ab-solute purity, of total faith in the other and ourselves. It is the moment (like Galileo's free fall of the bodies) that does not exist in our interactions. **But it can be the great EXPERIMENT of the really therapeutic interaction that we propose.** The other experiments, the other experiencing of the interaction will have flowed naturally from that decontaminated whole in that non-judgmental atmosphere or context in a interaction that is shorn of prejudices and is therefore one of total acceptance.

Is it difficult to do that? It is very much so because of the difficulty in getting into the Forest of Oblivion, especially as we keep the illusion that, without checking whether it is true, we consider ourselves to be healthy human beings free of prejudices and problems (see Alice Miller, notably 1993 and 1997).

Is that impossible? Of course not! On the difficulty of such oblivion, Merleau-Ponty once said that the greatest teaching of phenomenological reduction is that it is never complete. He therefore suggests to us the need to be always attentive to the possible residues of contamination, even when we put ourselves between brackets (as Husserl postulates), even in our best moments and our best interactions. Those are the moments in which the components of the interaction feel and actually are illuminated by one another.

We chase after that rare moment in the I/Thou relationship theorized by Buber.

Among those who had a facilitating attitude that is propitious to the appearance of that moment, we should remember Carl Rogers. He lived those relations often enough. He wrote somewhere that "there is no neutral human relation: they are always neurosis arousing or therapeutic." Of course he wrote that based on his long experience.

I imagine that Barry Stevens too gave that chance to those she related to, whether the interaction had the label of therapy or not.

A personal experience:

I have the unforgettable memory of moments to which I can certainly give the name of confirming interaction. A confirmatory, unconditional interaction with the other, a interaction free from any pedagogical residue, a interaction of real support for autonomy.

This happened during a group in which I was trainee/client. I plunged deeply into my history and, "vaccinated," I built a "cage" in order to protect myself from the therapist in charge and some members of the group. In that way, I managed to come into touch, in a more protected way, with the deepest pain and solitude, whose repression was unbearable. I was desperately alone.

At the height of despair, I noticed before me two large eyes (in the darkness in which I had fallen and that surrounded me, I did not want nor could see anything, but those large eyes were there). Today I know that they have come into my world, my cage, because they were simply there, intensely present, without projects or proposals. **They only (only?) welcomed me, took care of me.** They were really with me, without any intention to heal me or take away my pain. They had no intentions. They were eyes that were present, very present. Slowly they brought in Therèze A. Tellegen's shape. Her figure outlined itself. It also became present. It was a guarantee that I was not alone and that therefore I stood on ground, the necessary external support to let out that enormous pain. A pain that until then had been caught inside my chest and my throat. It would suffocate me and make me desperate.

Therèze is since long no longer among us, but her strong presence and particularly the image of those eyes on that day has never left me. They still keep me company at the crucial moments of my life.

It could be argued that we had been friends for a long time and that helped. Of course it did. Besides, it is not possible to know all the ingredients that come into an interaction, especially if that interaction is very intense. Many things may have had an influence on it, but that glance, **that strong presence at that crucial moment did not leave any room for doubt. It was what I needed in order to break through the old avoidance and come in touch with myself**, no matter how painful that in fact turned out to be (Therèze was not the official therapist on that occasion).

I lived another striking moment that I believe helps elucidate what happens on those really therapeutic occasions. It was during my professional specialization. This time it happened at Big Sur, California, in 1984.

That time my caretaker, midwife and travel companion and facilitator (unfortunately, this word has become very tainted) was Irma Lee Shepherd. I had got to meet her the day before, when she had arrived to be our "trainer" for that week.

I never saw her again, but her image, her figure and particularly **her strong undeniable presence have remained with me.** She has provided me with another, crucial liberating moment that has helped me to this day, seventeen years later, in my difficult and painful journey: to come into touch with my history, particularly that of my early childhood.

What do those two moments have in common that characterize them as so therapeutic?

I am grateful to those two exceptional women and bring them up here as examples. **I believe that they, at those moments, embodied in a concrete way what we propose as an attitude that is really therapeutic and that I have tried to expose and defend in this book.**

References:

Carrol, Lewis. 1994. *Through the Looking Glass and What Alice Found There.* Penguin, Puffin Books (First published 1872)

Miller, A. 1983. *For Your Own* Good (Hidden cruelty in child-rearing and the roots of violence), Farrar-Strauss-Giroux, NY.

Miller, A. 1994. *The Drama of the Gifted Child.* Basic Books, NY.

Miller, A. 1993. *Breaking Down the Wall of Silence.* (The Liberating Experience of Facing Painful Truth). A Meridien Book, Penguin Press: NY.

Maturana R., Humberto and Varela, Francisco. 1995. *The Tree of Knowledge.* First edition Scherz Verlag, Berna, Munique and Viena (1987). Brazilian edition, *Editorial Psy.*

Perls, F.S.; Hefferline, R.; Goodman, P. 1994. *Gestalt Therapy: Excitement and Growth in the Human Personality.* The Gestalt Journal Press: Gouldsboro, ME.

Varela, Francisco. "Connaître, Les Sciences Cognitives, Tendences et Perspectives." Portuguese edition: Instituto Piaget, Portugal.

"The final stage of experience, however, is not a subject of therapy: it is for a man to identify with his concern for the concernful and to be able to alienate what is unconcernful" (Perls et al. 1995, chapter XV, 14).

CONCLUSION

I do not know how much time I have expended on this book. Certainly it was sketched, though not on paper, many years ago.

Does it contain so much intellectual material that could take up all that time to elaborate? I do not think so.

Today, it seems clear to me that the delay was due mainly to the fright that the subject initially gave me and still does. It was also through "therapeutic" suffering that clarity and the dimensions of the problems to be faced have become clearer (as it has happened with several of our masters).

HUMAN EXISTENCE

To come into touch, to really listen or even think and write our own truth, the truth of our brothers and the naked truth of our daily life, our history, scares us as individuals and as citizens.

As you have observed, what underlies and serves as the supporting foundation for all the "therapeutic" points in the book is:

— the less I "push myself" or "am pushed," the more I "walk";
— the less others know what is best for me, the more I find out my true motives;
— the more they accept my defenses and resistance (carefully, as they are the result of creative adaptations), the less they make sense and the more they lose their force.

We behave in this way because **our sage knows that:**

— we are avoiding and why we are avoiding;
— that we do not understand because we do not want to or cannot know;
— that we do not see and why;
— that he, the sage, had to subordinate and place himself as dependant and why.

He has chosen the lesser suffering in the circumstances. At times, he had to "forget" many things in order to survive in the best possible way in that environment.

Conclusion

In order to be in touch again (or not) with repressed contents, with denied abilities, to develop again his perception of himself and the world, **he needs — it is fundamental for him — that the environment be one of acceptance without restrictions. In that way, the contact of the person with his owns sage has begun to be re-established again. It is only so that he will be able** to develop the conditions to go forward or not, to "cure himself" or not, with discernment and peace. **He knows and accepts** that he needs to use artifice to survive in the best possible way. That is why he will make use of it without developing a low self-esteem and sense of worthlessness. He will not feel guilty for having resource to those means because he also knows that he was compelled to develop them in order to deal better with control, coercion, manipulation or environmental violence.

It is therefore absolutely unnecessary, innocuous, besides dangerous and cruel, to try (against his philo- and ontogenetically developed system of resistance and defenses) to introduce in the experience of that person something that he has wisely repressed.

If he finds a context, a favorable space, he will wisely come again in touch or not at the time and rhythm determined by himself. This is the only way in which those repressed contents and those unfinished situations as well as new ones potentially dangerous (from his point of view) will be assimilated or excluded through creative integration that will thus only happen in the fullest freedom.

Our inner wisdom knew (and knows) what we have done, when we have repressed those contents; it also knows why we naturally inherited and individually developed our closedness, and how tight it is.

Certainly this same wisdom (if contacted and consulted) will also know when, how, to what extent and under which circumstances we will gently begin to open what is naturally and protectively closed.

APPENDIX I

Cognition and Existence Are One and the Same Thing. So, To Transmit It Has Its Own Way.

We do not see any difficulty in transferring these beliefs, beside all the other ones exposed in this book, to any other human interactionship. Or better, the difficulty is overcome to the extent that we do not deny it or the fear we have when about to face it and, of course, we have **begun to be** what we are talking about and trying to do.

In our approach, the distance between what we call psychotherapy and learning about what a human being might be and, consequently, ourselves, has been overestimated. Nobody deals with psychotherapy without learning more about themselves and about human beings in general; in the same way that nobody studies any basic way of conceptualizing the human being without feeling moved by it, without changing something in themselves somehow. Unless, of course, that learning happens only at an intellectual level; leading to what happens so often in psychotherapy: the person, then, explains coldly and with great competence their acts and ways of being as if they were talking about Martian butterflies: **without being involved and without the indispensable learning at an emotional level.**

HUMAN EXISTENCE

Here we continue to go against the flow of history and the establishment, also because we are amongst those who accuse the old dark pedagogy, autocratic and sceptic about the human being. That pedagogy is, therefore, based on a certain amount of previously established information about the Human Being's structures and how he perceives. Then it is about how he can or cannot learn. Not only our old pedagogy has been insensitive and forgetful of the differentiated development of each individual person as well as the problem of each person's intrinsic/ extrinsic motivation, but also, and because of its insensitivity, it harms the person in a useless, absolutely unnecessary, and cruel way as if running them over.

In this way, the difficulty in transmitting our practice is the same difficulty we have to face when practicing it: it is the lack of knowledge about the human functioning and as consequence the lack of trust, faith, in both ourselves and others (we should not forget therefore that this faith does not carry any trace of sentimentalism). We centre and focus on the problem (as in psychotherapy), but we are concerned about the "content, the basic concepts" and we forget about the person with their natural closeness, with their old protecting fears almost always untouchable and, for that reason, naturally suspicious of anything that might threaten their adjustments. This person has been compelled to develop such adjustments in order to survive. Adjustments that have, poorly or not, served a purpose until today. Then, not being respected, they will feed our defensiveness, our resistance and our structural closedness.

Cognition and Existence Are One and the Same Thing

The teaching methods, the pedagogy (official or not) which is in action everywhere and present in practically all activities that are dedicated to the transmission of anything are based on an old, outdated philosophy of controlling and coercion. That means it is totally deprived of the basic trust and the faith in the human being.

In this area, we also continue to behave in a way which is opposed to that of what we preach. Our discourse and our practice have conflicted in its essence: we talk about freedom for each and everyone of us but we have demands (for presence, for readings, for participation, for written works' presentation, evaluation etc.).

The practical result of that can only be the neurotic and increasing gap between intellectual discourse, attitudes and behavior. In formal education, it is very difficult to overcome this serious problem.

Of course we say that it is an increasing gap because (I insist on that which has been emphasized in the whole book) we formed/deformed (constructed) ourselves in an interactive process with this pagan culture that has no faith in the human being. We represent it. Unsurprisingly, the fact that we are always divided beings, always in some dichotomy, is reflected here in the pedagogical relationship which is what has caused most dichotomies in all cultures throughout history. Just as happened to us, we deform rather than help people to form themselves freely.

In our "training," the control and coercion, the idea of vertical relationships have been a current issue, not only as an existential attitude based on beliefs in the virtues of the cane, of the old pedagogy, but as a pure and simple exercise of power on the part of the "trainers" who, in this way, express their way of being in the world and their true beliefs. Maybe they take the opportunity to "pay back" the aggression that they suffered, and then they feed and perpetuate the thousands of vertical, disqualifying interactionships which started millions of years ago; interactionships which have generated wars that have lasted until today, as these have been further developed and perfected. In this way, teaching is an activity that became a way of molding, for it confirms the autocratic, controlling and coercing behavior we intend to substitute.

"Training" is a poor word that has a meaning very close to the meaning of the word "taming." For this reason, "training" should be thought of from the same perspective described above. Does it satisfy us as "trainers"?

We cannot forget the grandiosity that guided us to become a medical doctor, a psychotherapist, an educator, a priest or any other kind of "trainer," "savior." Such grandiosity is always carefully ready to defend itself by deviating or destroying any novelty, such as ours. For it can threaten its position of power and feeling of being superior.

What we would like to emphasize is that it could not be any different in the teaching activity: action changes radically with the new standpoint, the new philosophy, because the whole person is changed and their attitudes, preferences and taste are affected. This way, what we intend to do is to substitute the old vertical kind of relationship by a dignifying and efficient horizontal interaction.

When we are alert it is not difficult to perceive to what degree each person has been converted; changed to the beliefs proposed by our masters, observing their activities; no matter what activity (we expose ourselves through our actions). Rogers described the way of being of a person that we can call "converted." He described that way of being at different moments of his observation of the human being. See, for example, what Rogers & Rosemberg wrote, chapter XI (1977), under the title "The new person that is arising, a new revolution" or further in chapter XII (1978a).

Older research, like Adorno's about the authoritarian personality, shows us a radical difference in the ways of being and also interrelating with others that goes on when somebody is taken over by authoritarianism. **This authoritarianism, as we have seen many times, is the greatest sign of the lack of belief in oneself and others, and it prevails in our relationships.**

Again, we deal with very old ways of interacting. They are old in our history; they are extremely deeply rooted in us. Alice Miller´s second book (1984a) talks mainly about the manipulation of children as well as how badly treat-ed they are. It adopts the same questioning approach, and also tells us about finding out the essence of the philosophy of education that has been fostering educators' behavior since forgotten times. This way of interacting creates and develops our world and ourselves. The result is the creation, development and maintenance of a similarity of structures, which develop their own way of selective perception.

The resulting circularity feeds the continuity making difficult or even impossible the perception of the different, of the unusual, of the new.

It is clear for us that the problem is older than one may think but, historically, it is not easy to go further than she did (what today that is possible with the Biology's advances). But her findings were enough for us to evaluate the harm that an authoritarian relationship can cause, not only in formal education but in psychotherapy or in any other human interactionship.

These instances of lack of belief in the human being when he is free, are very old in our history and so very deeply rooted in us all. Although they interfere in our behavior, we can only perceive them when we can analyze with more freedom the reasons interacting with our actions. Every day it is clearer and more widely accepted that unless we specialists accept and face our own structural functioning, our own wounds and the authoritarianism caused and protected by them, we shall repeat the same features of a relationship that deforms, the

poisonous pedagogy which made us suffer and that we
will then pass on.

I insist on the importance of Alice Miller's work about
the etiology of violence in our societies. This author has
studied in depth how this process is repeated in our
history and how the fear and hypocrisy towards our own
violence (the violence we suffered and the one we perpe-
trate) makes us forget it, suppress it, deny it or, even
worse, disguise it with endless and often wise explanations and so protect it against those few who succeed to
see its monstrous face in our day to day life.

Maturana developed this concept and gave to it the name
of "structural coupling" (1999, 1987).

At the present moment in the history of our cultures, I
do not believe it to be possible for us to have a significant
change in the way of human interaction, which cruelly
spreads itself around the world reflecting on the way we
treat nature. However, I firmly believe and we have tried
to realize and accept (each one on their own pace) that
we are sceptic, and in general terms, autocrats and
violent in our most simple behavior, and in everyday life
attitudes. This happens at different levels, of course. It
is very well disguised so that our self-image may not be
affected. Only this disposition to be free from guilt and
the awareness that starts to exist from it can produce
results that might seem a miracle for those who have not
yet perceived the etiology of the change. For those who

have already become familiar with this etiology, the results are only logical and to be expected.

It is obvious and extremely clear that once a standpoint about human beings and the world has been really understood and taken on, this standpoint will interfere in all interactions. Although the repetition may sound tiring, we must say it again and again — especially if this standpoint comes against the main classic prejudices, as in our case, which have been developed for a long time in the history of our societies.

The subject we are dealing with is difficult to be faced as it affects us: **we are talking about ourselves, our families, our mothers, our beliefs and our most deeply rooted habits**; in short, about all our private stories and the history of humanity. That is why this subject touches us and presents us with a great dilemma: **if we do not allow this thesis to affect us we shall not understand it;** and if we do allow it to affect us, we might turn ourselves and our lives upside down like the hanged man in the Tarot card XII. **We are not learning about a theory and even less a technique: we are looking at a different way of existing and facing others, the world and ourselves**. This is something very difficult, painful and it takes a long time because this might unbalance us existentially, destructuring our equilibrium and adjustments both intellectually and emotionally.

Another problem which makes the teaching of our approach more difficult is that we are also dealing with

---

professionals who may have been working in the area for some time now and, for this reason, are inevitably in a hurry. The work is here to be done. The "clients" are in front of us with their pain. Pain is something that urges. (Running away from pain is a survival mechanism when we are in an emergency. Remaining in a runaway situation is alienating as Alice Miller has proved, mainly in 1993) We are eager to learn how to deal with this uncomfortable companion of our existence. **This drama brings us to the great risk of understanding it all only superficially and starting to apply knowledge not yet incorporated**. A lot has been written about the hurry in applying "procedures" acquired in a short period of time (Gary Yontef, 1981, and Isadore From, 1994, for example).

In spite of all this, if we look carefully even at some of our great masters, we will see that they have made unacceptable mistakes according to their own theories, but mistakes that are perfectly explained by their own structures and by the cultural hurry which makes us all victims, a hurry to act, to solve problems and therefore to interfere. We do not believe that the river will follow its own flow in the best way without interference. Or do we have to believe that our own intervention (and ourselves really) are so important?

These difficulties are expressed in **another apparent paradox: the more the understanding of a new concept is imposed upon us, the more it will remain, badly understood and not even close to being assimi-**

---

lated. This paradox is only apparent. The resistance, the defensiveness is the expected behavior when facing any imposition, even if it is self-imposed, or any other form of authoritarianism against ourselves perpetrated even, I insist, if the ones to do so are ourselves. Maybe this form of self-inflicted authoritarianism is more dangerous because we will always find a good way to give it an excuse.

We can become intellectuals, full of theories, sometimes excellent or brilliant, but our attitudes and our behavior will follow the inherited structures of operation. They will continue to obey the old belief, the old classic prejudices that, when threatened in their survival, will put up tough resistance and, not rarely, with great competence as if they were a wild animal in a corner.

In this way, control is kept and also, with our conservative ideas, the "non-confirmation" of those who are eager to learn. The learners themselves, through being pressured by the same prejudices which have been deeply rooted in themselves as well, think that it should be this way, that the control, the coercion should exist because "if I am not pressured I will not do anything." The disbelief and the established structures are defending themselves by all means and at all costs.

In order to learn about all sides of a new standpoint it is obvious, basic and indispensable that one may breathe in the environment where such standpoint is being

Cognition and Existence Are One and the Same Thing

transmitted, breathe the same air, the same trust and respect, the same faith that we want to transmit.

We should not underestimate, however, the difficulties, the resistance and the defensiveness in relation to the thorough understanding of this standpoint: let us remember the difficulties Carl Rogers, A.S. Neil and Paulo Freire had to implement their methods on a large scale. In spite of the fact that Neil sold more than a million of his *Freedom Without Fear*, and I do not know how many more copies of his other books; the general acceptance of Carl Rogers' thoughts and practice; and the fact that Paulo Freire was invited to lecture and run courses at the best universities around the country and abroad, in spite of all that, the resistance is still fierce.

In the same way as in psychotherapy, the natural resistance comes up everywhere. The most dangerous is the one disguised as a joining in that has been easy, fast and little reflected upon. **It is the most effective way of resisting: engulfing the new, the revolutionary in the old and conservative.**

We could say that this is a dishonest way of fighting against a novelty if we did not know that most people who behave in this way have no rational knowledge of what they are doing, not even the minimum awareness of that that they are doing. Or we could say that they are defending gently or with despair their own structures responsible for the continuity and safety of their identities. They are simply in contact with their self-preservation.

In this process their reason and their affect have lost sight of one another long ago. They have become (we have become) beings in a dichotomy, alienated and, therefore, we have little if any contact with our other side, the side of the no less vital need for growth, for the adoption of novelties. (Our abilities to take risks were drained in prior fights).

There is no guilty then, as we could not do any different because of the way we had to construct ourselves and the way we were brought up and educated, and very well "trained."

Yet, as resistance always has a meaning (accessible or not) and for this reason it cannot be refuted with impunity, for we have to deal with it in the most lovely and careful way as we can.

Not everything is a dark cloud: scientific development has been defeating "the politics of certainty" which is one of the supports of the autocratic way of thinking. In psychology, this way of thinking has suffered a blow recently (1996) when *Why We Do What We Do?* was published by Edward L. Deci. The book brought about decisive research results which were obtained from experiments, and they showed the positive consequences when people who are in powerful positions take an attitude that "supports autonomy." This attitude seems to have an influence over the intrinsic motivation of people in any relationship. That is to say that, worship-

---

ing freedom which was so difficult to accept and so easy to misunderstand in our autocratic societies, has found irrefutable scientific ground.

The more recent books coming from Neurobiology demonstrates that **it's impossible to invade an organism and help it.** (See Biology of Cognition's references).

All this encourages us but I repeat and insist: do not underestimate the strength nor the seductive ways of that autocratic, conservative and sceptic resistance, which will certainly be amongst us still for a long time. Furthermore, we should not forget that the historical process is slow as well as the structural changes, especially in what concerns that which is our area.

As we fight for interactionships, which are more horizontal, as the ones defended here so far, in a learning/teaching situation it is of great importance that our acts, attitudes be coherent with what we are transmitting. Without this coherence no increase in the amount of information will either make any sense or be effective. The democratic thought is transmitted only through democracy. Transmitting concepts, even "effectively," will not be any good if there is no harmony between the ways and the theory that we want to transmit. **On the contrary, there is no approach which has not yet realized that the rational explanation is the most efficient way to keep us untouched**, alienated from ourselves, from our emotions and problems that, inevitably, will affect our relationships including, obviously, the

---

learning/teaching relationship that is the subject of this appendix.

Looking around us and at ourselves it is easy to verify the statement in Perls et al.(1995) to the effect that "fundamental theoretical errors are invariably character-ological" and so "a basic error is not refuted" (chapter II).

Here too, we have to work respecting the differences, respect the learner's structure. We should work with and never against them. Otherwise, the individual structure will become even more closed.

Bearing this in mind, I did not work with training for many years.

We went back to the pretension of transmitting this way of facing and practicing our profession only in 1993.

What gave us the courage and support needed for trying it out was the conviction of the obvious, that the more we took the prescribed remedy, the less defensiveness we will face and the more the learning/teaching relationship will become like the one we preached and, of course, the better the results would naturally become.

This has demanded an extra indispensable effort from ourselves: the effort of being attentive and constantly vigilant in relation to our own behavior, and exchanging our impressions with members of the staff as often as we could. Not being concerned with the "we should not be the way we are." With this attitude, feed-back has been

Cognition and Existence Are One and the Same Thing

received without feelings of disqualification or inadequacy when we catch ourselves or others catch us acting in an autocratic way, because we share the principle that has been observed and proved that **all of us** carry old autocratic elements developed from our culture. So our structure couldn't be too different.

At least for a while and during our learning process (has it a final point?), we will continue to say one thing and do another.

The first step, then, was an opening class in which (I did not then know how long it would take) I tried to touch on the first notions of our theoretical basis, the purpose of the course as well as the difficulties and problems. In order to do that, we used, apart from our attitude aimed at fostering autonomy, the pragmatic contents as a stimulus for the creation of a group as democratic as possible. We had the intention of opening debates which were free and that could increase their freedom according to the atmosphere's growing.

This may seem an objective/means and it has been the real objective/end of the didactic experiment. As it is intellectually well known that, being in this atmosphere of participation where the hierarchy gives way to an open and fair dialogue, people who were characterologically prompted would interact in this way, find again their intrinsic motivation (suppressed by educational processes suffered until then). That motivation is the only real everlasting source of energy to search and learn that

we need. Biology of Cognition says that disturbing information cannot menace the continuity of the structural
functioning of any system, under pain that the menaced
system will close itself more and more.

Therefore, nothing is all that new really. The literature is
full of examples of such nature. Millions of books about
the effective-ness of freedom in education have been sold
(and certainly many have been read).

Nevertheless, as we have endlessly reasoned and proved,
this freedom is dangerously corrosive to any system that
has been established and stabilized, including ourselves.
And, as the means of communication are under the
control of those systems, the defensiveness, the resistance and the attacks against this freeing pedagogy form
a behavior expected by them (by us) because, and,
repeating it to exhaustion, no established system, no set
and defensive society can want the multiplication of
persons who are free and creative, people that will certainly undermine our old structures and society's own
autocratic and conservative structure.

So, in our course, we also face the expected inner resistance of each one including our own. In this way, we
have seen more or less what we have expected to face: a
lot of opposition. A small number of people (although
three times as many as in classic old training courses) go
into this fascinating but dangerous region of liberty **both**
intellectually and emotionally.

Cognition and Existence Are One and the Same Thing

A few privileged people already "live there" when they arrive. Others honestly believe they are getting there, but their behavior and a few comments they make show us that their beliefs and faith lie elsewhere.

The "sage" in these people seems to be preventing them from fully understanding what they are reading, listening or trying to live. He is keeping them away from a change that will cause them problems that they may not be ready to face.

In a third group of people, our ideals and attitudes being based on them do not get any further from the auditory barrier. This business of trust, faith, freedom for the human being cannot have and does not make any sense in their lives and, therefore, they cannot have and have never really had any sound contact with anything that happened around them. Many of these people, understandably and perhaps wisely, give up the study group.

Lastly, the group of people who feel they "have to" and "should" behave in a certain way. This group, obviously, goes until the end of the course, suffering along the course as they face ideas and attitudes that seem weird or unrealistic to them, if not absurd or counter-productive. Of course, these materials don't enter in their system. Their wisdom doesn't permit it.

Finishing my trying to pass on to you our way of transmitting what we think and do, we emphasize that **it only happens in the same way that a person can**

develop in psychotherapy: not being forced, not being controlled, not being coerced; but trying by all means to end any trace of despotism, of prepotence in the learning/teaching interactionship. Those traces may appear to us clearly or in disguise which has been developed by the hypocrisy of our society.

The only way out for us is to take increasing amounts of our powerful remedy made from respect to resistance, neuroses that we know that are functional and protective to the structure that maintains this person "walking," our remedy of real positive consideration to the person, of support for autonomy (freedom). All this leads to inevitable consequences of confirmation and self-acceptance that end up developing self-esteem and self-confidence, indispensable and sufficient for the person to have power over themselves, and also power to decide to change or not to change, to understand a new and disconcerting theory, or healthfully not understand it while there is no inner nor any outside support for doing so. That is, no indispensable support for understanding and living it.

APPENDIX II

A Mother/Child Relationship in Another Culture

I have talked many times about difficulties found in relationships, caused by the values and prejudices of our cultures. It seems that these difficulties are even more noticeable in the primary relationship between a mother and her child. As the episode that follows has always been present in my memory whenever I have dealt with these difficulties, I felt it would be fair and insightful to write this short appendix to tell the reader about it. A friend of mine, a doctor, a psychiatrist and psychotherapist, watched the following scene in a Xingu tribe:

Mother and son, both members of the tribe, were by the river bank. The mother was busy making some pottery. When my friend came near them, the woman had just finished making a vessel and had put it by her side. Her little son, who was around three years old, was playing next to his mother while she worked. The little boy saw the vessel that was ready, came nearer, got it in his hands and dropped the vessel on the floor smashing it to pieces.

His mother, placidly, got some more clay and started making another vessel, which had exactly the same

---

145

destiny as the first one as soon as it was finished. Again and again, another portion of clay, another vessel was made and another vessel was smashed on the floor. The woman from our culture, my friend, who was just observing the whole scene, could not remain silent anymore and spoke: "Are you going to make another one? Don't you see that he is breaking all the vessels that you're making?"

The answer was ready and easy to deliver: "If he has a need to break it, then I need to make it."

Knowing that we are almost always being tested on how much we accept others and how much we love them, especially by our children and our patients, I would like to ask: "How many of us (mothers, fathers, doctors, priests, psychotherapists etc.) who are the product, victims and carriers of the prejudices of our cultures; how many of us would have the indispensable inner conditions and the safe support of the environment to be successful in the test of the little inhabitant of the Xingu region?"

Appendix III

Individual X Society

The language we use in our everyday life is full of "thoughts" that point at "truths" that guide us, or even impose on us ways of thinking, or full of our attitudes and actions with respect to almost everything and over which we have no control nor do we have any awareness of what is happening with us and/or within the context we are in.

As an example of that, we hear that "a cane which is born crooked, will die crooked" (a piece of wood which was crooked at its creation will be crooked until its own end), or in a lighter vein, that,"we must straighten the cucumber while it is small" (we must avoid our children's misbehaving attitudes when they are still very small).

The dogmatic thought[*] that rules our prejudice and our beliefs will not encourage us, and it might even drive us away from reflecting upon the implications and develop-

---

[*] Any thought that refuses to put itself in question

---

ments of such expressions which may sound simple and harmless at first.

This way, we, conditioned human beings, move in a ready-made world, which has already been thought of by others. We do not perceive to what extent this world "ready-made" or "already thought" serves us or, to the contrary, if it coincides with what we would like to think or do about ourselves, about the others and the world that surrounds us, or if they all go towards an opposite direction.

Living in a dogmatic, authoritarian and prepotent society, since the beginning of our lives, we are not encouraged to question preconceived "truths." We are not stimulated to ask questions that might threaten the validity of these "truths" and, therefore, of our society itself. Simple questions such as: "Crooked seen from what parameter?"; "Crooked for whom?"; "Should it be straight to satisfy someone's needs ?"; "Doesn't it feel good being the way it is?"; "Who can guarantee that it will be crooked for ever?"; "Who is feeling uncomfortable about it being crooked?"

In Portuguese the words crooked — "torto" — torture — "tortura" — and the verb to torture, "torturar," come all from the same root and sound very much the same. Therefore, the pun that occurs here, in Portuguese, seems to be very appropriate since most of the "torture" we have to go through comes from the conflict between what we want to be and what others think we should be.

All our big and small wars start with this conflict and it is where we live all, or almost all of the time.

Society learnt, probably millions years ago, that "we must straighten the cucumber while it is very small." This postulate ended up developing an extremely efficient tactic/technique through which we are made crooked, moulded (or which crooks/moulds us according to its own parameters) when we are still too young and tender and, therefore, unable to defend ourselves.

Since we are very young, we are constantly discouraged from our curiosity, especially when it threatens to question some of the many untouchables taboos and/or dogmas of the system we live in.

At first, I thought of making a list of all these taboos and dogmas. However, I believe that it will be best if I ask you, the reader, to stop your reading and (together with other people, if possible) try to remember how many times you have been disrupted in the name of one of these prejudices when you were seeking for something. Preferably, add what kind of disruption, that is, how the authoritarianism worked on you: from "the purest, most simple and even honest" blow (which also harms, of course) until the most subtle and articulated manipulation: "It is for your own good"; "I do it out of love for you"; or "you are my favorite." Any seduction/ manipulation that left you confused, full of premature responsibility and each day more in the hands of those "powerful beings" who "think so much about you."

Modern psychology shows that **people who did that to us are just repeating what others did to them** (they may or may not know about it — in most cases, they do not perceive what they are doing), and in this way, unaware of perpetuating a vicious circle that is as old as humanity itself.

These eternal wars, generalized and so common, exist because there is a genuine conflict between the individual and the society they live in as it has been well pointed out by Gestalt therapy, chiefly Perls et al., 1995.

It is a genuine conflict because the same basic law in life rules both the person and the society, which is to preserve and survive.

The conditions for preservation grow as the person creates and develops his own potentials, and these will give them more self-confidence which is an indispensable and self-sufficient condition for them to risk or not, to question everything and everybody (also themselves) even further and with discernment.

However, this creative and developed kind of person is more and more able to think by herself or herself and, for this reason, they may be capable of unpredictable actions and attitudes ("anti-social?"). Therefore, this person becomes less controllable and trustworthy for a society that is insecure and needs (for its own guaranteed preservation and survival) people who are more predictable, stable, and especially those who are easily told what to do and that do not question its dogmas and prejudices, people who gave up their own individuality and have become a well adjusted piece in this big engine that is our society.

There is no doubt that the more insecure this individual and this society become (size does not matter — a nation, a company or just a family), because of their low level of self-confidence and faith in themselves, the more defensive, authoritarian and also overbearing they become, making repression more emphasized and . . . spreading and deepening the conflict.

Having this in mind, nothing sounds more natural than dreaming about perfect societies and individuals and from this unrealistic model we start to hide or defend at all costs that which seems to us to be "defects." Dreams and behavior easily seen in both individuals and in societies.

In spite of everything, this is the first and decisive step for us to consider ourselves (as well as our society, our family, our group) better than the others who, in their turn, look at themselves from the same point of view, the same needs and with the same self-indulgence: our race, our nation, our genre, our family and each and every one of us becomes better than those who are different.

These feelings and thoughts are the roots of intolerance and overbearing behavior, generating all the support to the infinite number of prejudices that rule us.

Therefore, nothing is more natural than some people trying to form, mould, or deform others according to their own image, a mutual behavior that obviously starts off the eternal misunderstandings, the defensiveness which makes us deaf, the conflicts that isolate us and the wars which eat us up.

Our possibility and hope of breaking this destructive vicious circle (and of saving ourselves?) lays on being more and more perceptive to the fact that, even when we are apparently completely involved in the drama of surviving at all costs — for sure, to a certain extent and level (intellectual or emotional) — we may be aware of what is happening. This awareness can cause us problems and suffering or, at least, an undefinable feeling of not being fine (e.g.: "I don't feel happy although I do not have reasons for that."). The fear of facing problems in general prevent us from looking into this pain or feeling that tells us we are not fine. This happens because if the situation becomes clearer, it will also become even more difficult to live in a make believe kind of situation and continue avoiding some solutions, which might be tough to face in the beginning. Even if this solution makes us feel powerless to change the status quo.

Nevertheless, we have to make this feeling less uncomfortable and in order to do this, one of the mechanisms we use to lessen the pain coming from these conflicts leads us to reinforce "escapism" and "denial," for instance, by resorting to myths: the myth of the paradisiacal childhood, the myth of the perfect relationship, the ideal man, the ideal woman; in short, beings and situations that are above any suspicion.

More frequently than we can imagine, we do need this escape; we need to deny what is around us especially, we insist repeatedly, when (as it happens with a little child) we do not have any power to change or to interfere in the context and/or process.

We can easily get to this obvious evidence by means of the most rigorous observations of what has happened around us and what has been happening during the whole history of human kind. This, we insist, to the extent which the researcher's fears and prejudices allow him to do so.

Is this inevitable and does this correspond to some "human nature"? Or is this the ordinary response of a human being facing demands above his own power, a great lack of means to satisfy their own basic needs?

It is good to know that the conflict still exists. One way or another, **we all resist total submission** to this because our other side, the human being that needs to develop his own individuality, his freedom, is also extremely strong. It may even seem that we have totally submitted, and yet the seed of individuality, the resistance to giving in remains in us. As Dostoievski described so well: even when we are under the most difficult conditions, this other side still lives in all of us (and it shows itself in some of us), this untamable side, this creative and nonconformist side that survives even under any oppression that might surround us.

Society, or any other institutionalized and fossilized system (even each one of us when we are taken by our rigidity) has this side that questions everything but tries to suffocate it by all means, and history is full of extreme examples of this attitude. The oldest that comes to my mind is the one about Socrates who taught his pupils to think with rigor and was condemned to death by the allegation that he was corrupting the youth. Recently, Carl Rogers was accused of the same thing, which shows us that this old conflict is still alive and threatens those many who insist and, despite everything else, still fight for a better world.

APPENDIX IV

The Practice of Ethics as Self-Help

Ethical behavior is usually understood as being restricted to a helping stance in conformity with some moral, pre-established philosophy. This last accredits its author before an earthly world or a heavenly one. There is therefore a third "person" and/or intention involved in the relation. At the very least, there is the expectation of some beneficial return coming from outside the author of the action.

This piece however centers on the effects and the automatic return received by the author of the ethical attitude, independently from interference from other factors beyond one's own attitude. That is, it emphasizes that ethical behavior is in itself highly beneficial for those who practice it. It does not depend on possible external rewards, as once we practice it we trigger internal processes that are healthy for our internal physical, psychological and spiritual health.

Ethical action thus understood is, in this way, more closely linked to an existential wisdom that brings us closer to "our natural biological altruism . . . that is a purely biological force common to all social beings"

(Maturana and Varela, 1995, page 23) than any norma-
tively adequate behavior.

It is **"fazer o bem sem olhar para quem,"** or to do good
to everyone. This is a saying from our commonsense or
our age-old wisdom (this last has inspired the behavior
of many for millenia, even though those many make up
only a minority in our societies).

This is behavior and a kind of attitude that is diametrically opposed to the hasty individualistic race of most of
us. In this race, our actions are geared to obtaining
immediately or ultimately some advantage for us. This is
our "banking spirit," as Paulo Freire would put it. It is a
spirit that is always attentive to possible and visible
immediate gains every time we make a move, even if only
in thought.

It is the "give and take" that motivates and moves the
vast majority of our attitudes and actions. The belief in
this interactional mercantilism is so deep and well-rooted and unconscious that we often find that we can even
make a deal with God as when we say that **"quem dá
para os pobres, empresta a Deus"** ("Who gives to the
poor people, lends to God").

I do not know, nor do I know whether it is possible to
know, when and how this competitive/defensive/mer-
cantilist and accounting-related way of relating with
each other, the world and ourselves began to take root in
human behavior. Its origin gets lost in the distant past.
That is why it is even considered to be part of human

"nature," even though this has always been denied by the minority of people mentioned above. This is a denial that has been gathering power in the scientific domain notably in the last three decades from the neurobiological discoveries (see the works of Humberto Maturana and Francisco Varela, as well as the extensive bibliography about the most recent research available in their books).

What is easily observable is the intensity and the large degree to which we are put under pressure (and even forced) to "mercantilize" ourselves. This happens notably through dear ones who do not want to see us "left behind" in the endemic and cruel competitiveness that has taken root in our societies. In it we have to be "winners" in whatever we undertake. It does not matter whether we have any intrinsic motivation for the struggles that we are forced to face. This generalized practice leaves to a minority of researchers and scientists, distant from the general public, the work of evaluating the costs and possible consequences of such a way of being with others, with the world and even with oneself.

The media kept by the immediate interest of a small and powerful section of society has brilliantly played the role of promoter and keeper of this mercantilism geared to immediate profit.

In spite of the harmful and undesirable effects of this individualistic radicalization for the health of individuals and society being obvious and visible, most of us stubbornly ignore them and/or seek the reason for its effects elsewhere, like somebody who has lost an object in a dark room and next searches for it in a lighter and less charged place "where it is easier to find it." Find exactly what? Certainly not what we have exactly lost, but something more desirable for our Narcissus.

That is what we have done, for example when we look for the roots of growth of alcoholism, of drug-addiction and violence. These are certainly found in the dark and toxic rooms of our interactions. However, we stubbornly look for them in places distant from our responsibility and less compromising to our image and self-esteem. These are places that are considered to be "lighter" because more distant and therefore requiring less involvement and personal risk. To put it more incisively: we do not want or do not have the courage to look for them in the dark alleys of our toxic daily form of dealing with each other in our interactions. We do not even want to look dispassionately how we treat ourselves.

The cost of that avoidance/denial/blindness has been extremely high.

And it is painful to notice that that high cost we have paid and the consequences we have had to bear with are not inevitable. That is so because those competitive, aggressive and defensive kinds of anti-life behavior do not correspond to any human nature.

For millenia, the minority that has behaved in a way opposite to the dominant one — being therefore not interest-driven, not seeking immediate gain, not egotistical and not mercantilist. This minority has shown us their well-being, their physical and mental health, their peacefulness and happiness. What is their secret?

The consequences of those two opposite ways of relating to each other and existing have implications whose degree and scope go beyond the current comprehension in our sciences. However, these have, in the past few decades, already detected and measured important response-related physiological, psychological and spiritual differences. These are **triggered off** in live systems, notably in human beings, when they are affected by one of those ways with which we deal with ourselves and/or are dealt with by others.

The richness, complexity and subtlety of our interactions are wider and much more encompassing as we "have a readiness-for-action adequate for each specific lived situation" (Varela, 1999, page 9).

However, trying to make the matter more palatable, for the purpose of this piece we will restrict ourselves to two organic reactions of live beings. These have already been widely studied and measured (notably in human beings) by Western researchers. These are also the concern, focus and interest of activities from the East such as, for instance, the practice of meditation.

I talk about all the organic reactions **triggered off** in us when for instance the environment is fully favorable and caring, one of "unconditional positive consideration" (as Carl Rogers used to postulate), one of "confirmation" (according to Martin Buber). This caring, loving, accepting, mild climate leads us **(triggers in us)** a set of reactions that scientists denominate "relaxation response." This, besides being visible to any observer, can and has been measured (especially by cardiologists and oncologists) through physiological changes shown, among other kinds of measurement, in the encephalogram, in the psychogalvanic reaction (electricity on the skin), in the alteration in the production of adrenaline, noradrenaline, in the change in heartbeat, oxygen intake, etc. That is, there is an improvement in the general functioning of the individual and the whole organism can "surrender" itself because it feels as safe as a little animal in its den. It is not paradoxical that there is a general improvement in the person and her reactions come to be quicker. Therefore, his ability to survive well is increased by the general improvement in the reactivity of the system.

There is a set of reactions triggered when we are and feel fully cared for, without even a modicum of a feeling of external threat or external control and oppression (whether these are ingrained, suggested, perceived, felt or intuited). In opposition to that set of reactions there is a set of **triggered** and opposite reactions that we call a **readiness for attack/flight reactions.** That is when we tense up, our hair is on end, with popped-out eyes and an exacerbation of all reactions described in the last paragraph, besides many other symptoms that still escape our immediate observation. That is, there is an intense preparation for defense or attack, when accumulated energy is obviously burned up and there is great physical and emotional waste.

"The reactivity of the nervous system articulates with the reactivity of the glandular and immunological systems" (Maturana, 1999, page 329).

These two antagonistic sets of organic reactions have been developed by live beings through millions and millions of years. They are absolutely necessary in order to help us deal competently with the most varied and different existential situations in our daily lives. Perhaps it might be easier to imagine this kind of functioning in its purest form in the unstable and dangerous daily life of our most primitive ancestors. However, it possible (and not so difficult) to observe these states of well-being and being unwell in our most current and "normal" family, professional and even playful relations. It is enough that we sharpen our attention a little in order to notice (and register) those mute little wars that seep through and instigate the some times sudden changes in behavioral responses even when these show up wearing the masks of kindness and good intentions.

We stress that those are specific responses developed by our age-old wisdom so that we can face up to the most varied and specific existential situations.

Nonetheless, the world has changed. Great predating animals have become extinct. Interactions have become more complex and subtle, and so has society. Thus, dangerous and even loving situations have become ever more difficult to notice, discern and evaluate with clearness. The beast living in our surface has been tamed, but man remains man's worst enemy. Only, it is an ever darker enemy, ever more disguised, shrewd, cunning, hypo-critical and even treacherous. Of course, our inner sage has developed a system of responses to that new situation. He has psychologically armed himself as never before and we live in fear of all and everyone. The popular saying that "in a river full of piranhas alligators swim on their back" expresses this feeling and attitude of general insecurity that is deeply rooted in our cultures.

This frame of mind leads us to kinds of behavior that are similar to that of the porcupine. This last, aware of its fragility, swells out with its protective thorns and does not perceive what its thorns trigger in the world around it. I do not know whether he, like ourselves, complains of solitude and isolation that are a result of its own system of defense (thorns, armors, caskets) and the limited existential spaces that are left when we live "in safety." As for us, we have developed one of the great human dilemmas: for fear of being hurt, we isolate ourselves from one another and next complain about loneliness.

Today it is known that most of us receive witch-like, ambiguous messages of contradictory or conditional love (love that is not love) or even rejection (whether explicit or not) since our time in a womb. (See, among many others, the very important work by Alice Miller. To my mind, hers is the most profound, incisive and rigorous research, reflection and analysis on the roots of so much defensiveness and violence).

The Practice of Ethics as Self-help

In that ambiguous and obscure climate, we cannot completely relax. Everyday our state of tension bothers us more. They drain up our power and undermine our well-being.

Everyone of us, to a greater or lesser extent, are also ambiguous and even incongruous in our way of relation because of the dubiousness and incongruity of the environment where we have developed and made ourselves. The overwhelming majority of us has been raised and lived with an insufficient amount of love and acceptance. (We are loved and confirmed on condition that we do and be what is desired and prescribed for us. Of course, that is not the nourishing and unconditional love that we need for our differentiated and unique development).

With the growing complexity and ambiguity in our interactions and the resulting difficulty in evaluating even what is happening around us, it becomes ever more difficult to develop the most adequate kind of response for each moment. In that way, we develop an exhausting way of being and being in the world that Perls and others (1994) have called "chronic low-tension imbalance" (chapter II).

Maturana writes that many pathologies come up in *rupture between coherence and circumstance* [italics mine] . . . and that "there are many diseases that are in truth distortions of the harmonious flow of the immunological system (1999, page 330).

Due to that contextual ambiguity we cannot adequately relax in our relations (even in our most current ones). On the other hand, if we were to be permanently in a state of "readiness," always attentive and ready to respond to all provocation, disqualification, nagging and back-stabbing with which we are always tormented, we would also trigger against us (besides internal processes) more aggressions, in a never-ending wasting until our forces were exhausted in little time. In that way, we would also be at the mercy of events and/or specialists as unfortunately many of us are when, for instance, we are taken by the panic syndrome.

Nothing is more normal, fair and obvious that we would gradually lose our Faith and Trust in others, the world and ourselves ("what have I done wrong?" is one of the questions with which we torment ourselves). The nebulousness of the situations, the distrustful context, dubious interlocutors have developed our own confusion and lack of clarity. A cruel and growing vicious circle has established itself: the more dubious the situations, the more dubious we become. We nourish the circle. We become either ingrained aggressors or submissive hypocrites. Our behavior becomes ever more like that of a street bully. We distrust all and everyone. That makes us into the overbearing/fearful or defensive/guilty/compulsive that walk around.

In that way, the vicious circularity, that cruel cybernetics, has been working against us. It is almost impossible to stop this harmful and anguish-ridden process. It is also very difficult to slow it down: it would be like trying to suddenly stop a heavy vehicle on a rainy day.

In spite of being ever more aware of the toxicity of our interactions, my optimism continues to grow as I think about the future of humanity. For me, that is not a product of a naive romanticism, but of solid scientific and philosophical convictions.

That optimism has been inspired and fed for decades by those who have always believed (and have reflected, as they have theorized, preached and exerted themselves) in the possibility of living in greater peace, harmony, love and happiness. That optimism continues to state that that predatory behavior that has taken root in our cultures does not correspond to any human nature. That has been increasingly confirmed by recent scientific research, notably neurobiological one.

Thus, against all evidence from merely confirmatory statistics that generalize as "human nature" a cannibalism that rules our actions, we can already state, on a more scientific basis, that the Human Being is in his innermost essence and wisdom collaborative. In this way, he is concerned with others, even with his concern is more visible in a pure state only in extreme situations as, for instance, when you "rescue a baby" (the baby's example is given in Varela, 1999, pages 27 and 67). If you have had a similar experience you will remember how you felt (and, with the knowledge at our disposal now, you can imagine how that felt well-being was beneficial to your physical, psychological and spiritual health). That is, **your own ethical action already triggers in you, automatically, countless beneficial results.** In particular, it helps you and those with whom you live to disentangle themselves from malefic preconceptions and evil relational habits to which we have been chained for millenia.

Therefore, we cannot forget that, if we wish to further any improvements, that "state of grace" in itself **triggers in us a network of reactions** that is extremely beneficial to our health. That, in its turn, reinforces that first "state" and so on and on. It establishes a circularity that is self-nourishing and will feed the well-being of all. It will contaminate in a benefic way our environment, thus making it into an ally for the strengthening of that positive cybernetics.

That behavior, as it wells up from our innermost soul, is spontaneous, unintentional, non-deliberate. It is a "wholesome," global and embodied network of responses. **It is therefore free from any calculation**. It already exists in our system, even though it is more dormant in some of us and less so in others. What is important is that we do not have to invent it, much less have somebody set it up in us. For its development it is enough that there should be a favorable context (see especially chapters 4, 5, 6 and 8).

It is not too much to insist on the reminder that our mechanism works with the same efficaciousness and speed, but in the opposite way, when we are attacking or being attacked in any way, even if the attack is against ourselves or it goes unnnoticed by others (or others are unaware of it).

In that privileged frame of mind that follows an ethical (clean and unintentioned) action, we become more than we usually are. Even our critical thought develops and sharpens itself. That enables us to take out from their deep trenches some of the stepmotherly and anti-human assumptions about ourselves and our relations. These have been transmitted to us and have put down roots inside us since a long time. We have therefore been chained to them since living memory.

Therefore, because it is a natural attitude in our very being, our own way of organization, we do not need a baby to fall into a well in order to have the chance to recover, develop and exercise that innate human solidarity that leads us to well-being and a better life. **It is enough that we remain attentive and vigilant as to how we have been treating each other and ourselves**. That is, to the kind of behavior that has been filling up our existential space. We should observe to what degree human solidarity takes place around us or not. Unfortunately, this search also leads to a growing awareness of a deeply rooted defensiveness that does not allow or makes difficult the perception of any act of good will seeps through our interactions. That defensiveness usually leads us to mistrust the possible intentions of those who are practicing it, disqualifying them and inverting, in that way, the cybernetics that started out in good will. That is cruel, inhuman and suicidal for all of us. It only happens at all because our Faith and Trust in others, the world and even ourselves have already been profoundly compromised a long, long time ago.

This lack of trust is reinforced because *"that loving solidarity and the possibility of concern with others, present in all humans, is usually mixed with a sense of ego and is thus confused with the need to satisfy one's ambitions for acknowledgment and self-validation. Those categories include 'a lot of good people' around us."* (Varela, 1999).

In that case, of course, we only manage to cheat our rational opinions as well as those who, like us, have become used to live "as if," in make-believe, in seeming and not in being. The wisdom of our organismic organization and our old inner sage do not take notice of those surface operations and only **trigger** the benefic inner and social processes **when there is really no trade-off involved**. It does not matter whether the author of the action has any awareness of his trading-off.

I must insist that inside that ethical attitude, in real and clean human solidarity, there is no place for the "as if," no place for cheating, even if it be the painful self-cheating wisely developed by ourselves in order to survive better in unfavorable environments where they have a meaning and function (and only there). Age-old organismic wisdom does not take part in the ingeniousness of the stratagems developed by itself in order to ensure our immediate survival in hostile environments. It **knows** the reasons that have led it to develop them. It also knows the costs it has paid for resorting to them. Thus, when we free ourselves from rational assumptions and allow that wisdom, free and uncommitted, to take over the process of decision-making, it will carry it out with prudence and insight.

Overburdened strictly rational wisdom uses to (needs to) selectively "forget" many things, a lot of accumulated garbage.

I insist that **there is no way of cheating that wisdom that has been developed for millions of years by human beings**, and perhaps for billions of years by simpler nervous systems that have predated us. Nonetheless, our cultures, notably our arrogant and overbearing western civilization, stubbornly believe that they can control, manipulate and distort that deep nature.

For centuries we have tried to monitor, "improve," modify or "cure" others without success. Those attempts always happen from some pre-established pattern. And as those "others" are also always trying, from other also pre-established "truths," to do the same to us, a "state of war" has been set up and it goes on in our lives. It hinders the indispensable and healthy respect that we all want and that is indispensable for our personal development and that of our interactions.

Therefore, the only visible and possible way out is to try and learn to imitate those sages who have already noticed and lived harmoniously with that wisdom. They are many (even though they are a minority in our cultures, notably in Western culture). Certainly any of us can be in touch or have access to the thought and way of life to some of them. It is easy to ascertain **how the ethics of their lives is beneficial to themselves as well as to those who come near them.**

It is likely that, due to yet another of those countless assumptions ("that live in us in the dimension of oblivion without knowing themselves to be forgotten" [Bornheim 1983]) or some scientist or cultural vice that rule us, **we Westerners hoped that science would come to that wisdom**. Some major scientists have got there. We will come in contact with their findings. Will we then concern ourselves more with each other, ourselves and the destiny of all?

References:

See bibliography of Biology of Cognition, Alice Miller, Gerd Bornheim and Paulo Freire (quoteds); and

Miller, A. 1983. *For Your Own Good* (Hidden cruelty in child-rearing and the roots of violence), Farrar-Strauss-Giroux, NY.
Miller, A. 1994. *The Drama of the Gifted Child.* Basic Books, NY.
Miller, A. 1993. *Breaking Down the Wall of Silence* (The Liberating Experience of Facing Painful Truth — A Meridien Book, Penguin Press: NY.
Maturana R., Humberto and Varela, Francisco.1995. "The Tree of Knowledge" — First edition Scherz

Verlag, Berna, Munique and Viena (1987) — Brazilian edition, *Editorial Psy.*

Merleau-Ponty, Maurice — "Les Cours de Sorbonne, Les Sciences de L'homme et la Phénoménologie" — Centre de Documentation Universitaire — 5, Place de La Sorbone, Paris V, France.

Mc Wilhams, Peter. 1976. *The TM Program: A Basic Handbook* A Fawcet Crest Book.

Varela, Francisco. "Connaître, Les Sciences Cognitives, Tendences et Perspectives" , without date. Portuguese edition: Instituto Piaget, Portugal, no date.

- This theme was exposed in the Deputy Chamber, Brézil, in Augusto, 25, 2001. After that, the TV Câmara has transmitted it several times to all over the country.

What is Gestalt Therapy from This Perspective?

For Gestalt therapy we are beings that make themselves in their relational experiences. We bring to our individual development, as a hereditary burden, our potential, our wisdom developed and accumulated by our ancestors and the ancestors of our ancestors. With all this wealth of possibilities/potentialities we have not been born pre-determined to be either murderers or angels, dominators or dominated, victimizers or victims or anything else. The essence of our organization (including our nervous system) does not allow us to be determined.

We develop pre-existing potentialities in our interactions with environment. This can have an influence in the **triggering off** of internal processes of change that can lead to adaptations. The environment however cannot directly determine any change. The feeling of identity of our organization of beings that self-create themselves would become threatened in its continuity, essence and way of being in the face of any attempt at external interference. **It might trigger off** reactive processes of defense and self-preservation by putting us in conflict. There is a conflict because we need that way in order to survive. The impasse thus created will have to be solved by the creative integration of those opposites. Obviously, it will be an integration that is only possible within the limitations of each circumstance and moment in that specific relation.

In this way, we develop the being that we are (that we shape/misshape) in our possible relations. Our first relations are the most important ones, as, the more tender, and in need of external support, the more unpro-tected, the more we are subject to adaptation without integration. In order to self-preserve in the best way possible and at the same time protect our own identity, we begin to shape/build our way of being already in the intra-uterine relation (the beginning of our ontogenetic development).

Again, our behavior is therefore not pre-determined **("pau que nasce torto permanece torto"** — "a branch that is born crooked will remain crooked") is therefore not our belief. We insist that we create ourselves, build our own characteristics, both in favorable environments as well in unfavorable ones. That makes us so similar to other people and so different from others.

So, we are basically (we insist) the result of creative adjustments, of arrangements and cunning that came up between our potentialities developed throughout millenia and the resources and environmental possibili-ties to respond to our fundamental need for growth without threat to our self-preservation. There-fore we have in us the beginning, a great and complex wealth of potentialities/abilities needed and sufficient for our development and our formation. This happens in the best way possible within the possibilities that came up during our personal history.

When there is a sufficient amount of Faith, Trust and Love in our relations we develop in the best way possible for us, for others and the world; when those conditions do not exist (as is usually the case), we do our best. We have an inner sage in charge of our process of decision-making. Our decisions have reasons that usually escape our conceptual reason.

The Human Being therefore has all the instruments that he needs in order to develop in a healthy and happy way (and to provide the same to others). In order to do that it is enough (like in the case of a good seed) to have freedom (external support for autonomy) and to live in favorable environments. He must be loved and accepted as he is in those environments. He needs to be trusted (the ground does not require the seed to be what it is not).

The problem is that the great majority of those relations in which we form ourselves do not trust our inner wisdom (in our old sage, as Perls would put it). Because they are in the service of overbearing and insecure societies, it is forceful, controlling and punitive.

That attitude on the part of almost all societies, besides taking away from us the possibility of developing ways of being different from those preached by them and their agents for control, tries to take away from us the power of subjects/agents of our own development. That inherent power is indispensable for us to exist according to our essence of a being that creates himself.

Taking into consideration those essential ways of "being" and "functioning" of the Human Being, we propose a liberating therapy, a therapy that only (only?) gives us support for our autonomy to choose and follow our own paths. That proposal has already been presented and defended by some modern psychotherapists.

My version of that way of relating to each other is in the final chapters of my book *Existência >> Essência — Desafios Teóricos e Práticos das Psicoterapias Relacionais*, published by Editorial Summus, São Paulo, 1998.

INDEX

---

www.ingramcontent.com/pod-product-compliance
Lightning Source LLC
Chambersburg PA
CBHW030651270326
41929CB00007B/303